PORTRAIT OF WILMSLOW

Alderley Edge & Handforth

Ron Lee

SIGMA
Leisure

Published by Sigma Leisure - an imprint of
Sigma Press, 1 South Oak Lane, Wilmslow, Cheshire SK9 6AR, England.

British Library Cataloguing in Publication Data: A CIP record for this book is available from the British Library.

ISBN: 1-85058-556-3

Typesetting and Design by: Sigma Press, Wilmslow, Cheshire.

Printing and cover design by: MFP Design and Print

Cover photographs: from top to bottom – Nether Alderley Mill, south of Alderley Edge; staff restaurant by the trout lake, Refuge Assurance head office, in the grounds of Fulshaw Park, Wilmslow (courtesy of Refuge Assurance plc); Grove Street, Wilmslow, in the early 1900s; Wilmslow & Alderley Edge Gas Co. lorry, 1930.

Acknowledgements: The author wishes to thank the following who have helped in supplying information or who have supplied or loaned photographs and illustrations: The Picture Place Ltd; The Sunday Telegraph; Cheshire Life; the Wilmslow Express Advertiser; Mr M D Hobkirk; the Trustees of the British Museum; Mr R C Turner; the Rector of Wilmslow, the Rev P J Hunt; Mrs June Woollam; Imperial Chemical Industries; the Basil Jeuda Collection; Mrs A R Faulkner; Mr Albert Hartley, former Chief Librarian, Mrs Elaine Street and the staff, Wilmslow Library; Mrs E Banks, Alderley Edge Library; the staff, Handforth Library; the Ford Motor Company; Refuge Assurance Company; Miss B Jones; Mr and Mrs J E M Reeman; Mr J Hewitt; Umbro International Ltd; Mr R J H Couchman; Mr J Stansby; Technical Services Department and Diane Smith, Macclesfield Borough Council; Messrs Wimpey.

Preface

"It is better to excite the reader's judgement briefly, rather than to inform tediously."

This succinct pronouncement by the philosopher Francis Bacon sums up the author's thoughts admirably. It is said that in politics there is only one crime worse than being wrong and that is being dull. The adage may well apply to history. There must be thousands of people who found school history lessons as boring as a party political broadcast, simply because they were not presented in an interesting way.

This book aims to present the changing face of Wilmslow, and its neighbours Alderley Edge and Handforth, in a combination of fascinating anecdotes and unique pictures, many published for the first time. It takes us from the time Lindow Pete met his gruesome death about 2,000 years ago, right up to the present day, and on into the future. There was the period when Wilmslow was a thriving textile town; the days when lodging house keepers were obliged by law to clean the bedding "From time to time"; the desperate months when the townsfolk fought off a takeover bid by Manchester. In Alderley there is the fairytale background to the Edge; in Handforth the history of the Hall and the strange prisoner of war camp.

It is a history that is both enjoyable and informative, without being tedious.

Readers who wish to discover more about the area may find the following books useful:

Cheshire: *East Cheshire*, Earwaker; *History of Cheshire, George Ormerod*; Kelly's *Directory of Cheshire*; *Directory of Cheshire Towns*; *Bagshaw Gazetteer*; White's *Directory of Cheshire*; *Old Cheshire Churches*, Raymond Richards; *The Place Names of Cheshire*, J. McN. Dodgson.

Wilmslow: *Wilmslow Graves and Grave Thoughts of Wilmslow*, Alfred Fryer; *History of Lindow*; *Recollections of William Norbury*; *The Story of Wilmslow*, Howard Hodgson; *Pleasant Pastures*, Walter Lazenby and Fred Morgan; *The Wilmslow of Yesterday*, Wilmslow Historical Society; *The Old Community of Wilmslow*, Howard Hodgson; *The Bog Man and the Archaeology of People*, Don Brothwell; *The Gregs of Styal*, Mary B. Rose; *The Gregs of Quarry Bank Mill*, Mary B. Rose; *Wilmslow Past and Present*, Andrew Pearson.

Alderley Edge: *The Stanleys of Alderley*, Nancy Mittford; *The Ladies of Alderley*, Nancy Mittford.

Handforth: *Handforth through the Ages*, F.E. Heusel.

Ron Lee

Contents

Chapter 1: Face from the Past

Thumb carefully through the definitive pages of the Domesday Book and you will find, perhaps surprisingly, that Wilmslow did not rate a mention. The scribes sent out by William the Conqueror in 1086 to report on soil cultivation, values of mills, fishponds and cattle, probably took one look at the acres of oozy bog and marshland, with its 50 or so worthy inhabitants, and went on their way.

Down through the centuries Wilmslow remained largely undistinguished. Perhaps it had some claim to importance, if not fame, as a minor cotton centre at the turn of the 18th century, but for years after that it languished as a mainly depressed, working class town.

In more recent times, as a modern day commuter town, it stepped up into the executive class, but it was no more significant than Watford or Widnes. Then, on 1st August, 1984, it all changed, thanks to an elderly chap called Pete.

Suddenly Wilmslow was famous. Perhaps not of Pompeii proportions, but it was definitely on the map. Andy Mould was working at Lindow Moss on a peat excavating machine when he suddenly spotted what appeared to be a piece of wood. On closer examination it proved to be a human foot. Other parts of the body were found and removed to the mortuary at Macclesfield hospital. As police were considering setting up a murder inquiry, they soon discovered

This is the face of Lindow Pete, complete with red moustache and red beard, as reconstructed by scientists from the British Museum. Little did he realise when he met his gruesome death by garrotting, that he would turn up 2,000 years later as a 'pin-up' in several books and as a TV celebrity. Scientists calculate the age of a find by using a carbon dating technique. Humans absorb particles of radioactive carbon from the atmosphere. This level falls after death. Scientists know the original level and rate of decay and estimate the age by comparing the two. The method is accurate to within a few hundred years.

1

The scene on Lindow Moss after Pete's body was found. Workers and archaeologists search the site for more remains. The hunt began when a workman removing peat examined what he thought was a piece of wood. It turned out to be a human foot. A few years later, more remains were recovered.

that the chances of finding the killers were pretty remote – the victim, nicknamed Pete Marsh by the press, had met his gruesome end some 2,000 years ago.

(By chance, Andy Mould had been involved in another bizarre discovery of a woman's head in May, 1983. Police decided to look further into the disappearance 13 years earlier of the wife of a local man, Peter Reyn-Bardt. When questioned, he confessed to her murder and was later sentenced at Chester Crown Court. The woman's skull eventually turned out to be 1,700 years old!)

Pete had been garrotted, beaten about the head by a blunt instrument and had a blade stuck through his neck – definitely a case of foul play. He was naked apart from an armband of fox fur, his hands clasped together, possibly in prayer, and was almost certainly the sacrificial victim of a ritual execution.

Most of the lower half of his body was not recovered because the peat cutting machine had sliced through his bones. They were found eight feet below the surface, perfectly preserved by peat acids. The remains were pieced together by forensic experts from the British Museum and they came up with a profile that would have astonished even Sherlock Holmes, famed for his elementary deductions.

Pete was thirty-ish with mousy hair, red moustache and beard. His fingers were well manicured, suggesting he was a sort of "white collar" chap, and he had just eaten a meal of unleavened bread. Pete was the subject of two Q.E.D. television programmes, Prince Charles turned up to look at him in a London exhibition and 150,000 visitors stared at him at a splendid exhibition at Manchester Museum. That is where the great northern public would have liked him to stay. Tatton MP Neil Hamilton backed a campaign to keep him, but Pete was again crated up and whisked back to London. Another example of what is known as the North-South divide.

If the ancient bog feller could have undergone a kind of metamorphosis and joined us on a nostalgic tour of the area today, he would have been as bemused as his 1987 film counterpart, *Crocodile Dundee*, who was transported from a primitive swampland existence in the Australian outback to a ritzy life among American skyscrapers. Not all the

Lindow Pete, in the guise of the then Labour Leader Neil Kinnock, was used as a jibe at the Labour Party in this Sunday Telegraph cartoon in October, 1984. At the time, Mr. Kinnock was having problems at the party's conference over the long-running miners' strike. (Also in the cartoon, left to right, are: Michael Foot, James Callaghan, Dennis Healey, Gerald Kaufman, Peter Shore and Roy Hattersley.)

changes have been for the better, but a few people would dispute that Wilmslow is now a pleasant place in which to live.

Pete might have wondered why Wilmslow's original so-called by-pass went right through the town centre and pondered on whether the new one would prove to be a blessing or a blight. (Further thoughts – see Chapter 11.)

Back to the beginning, and the inevitable question: How did Wilmslow get its name? Etymologists say it originally meant Wighelm's Mound and may have had something to do with a landowner called William De Wilmslow who was around in 1260. However, as no-one seems to know who Wighelm, or William, was, it can perhaps be discarded under the heading of Useless Trivia. (Hopefully this will be the first and last such item). Historians will tell you that the town's ancient name was Wilmesloe, but the English Place Name Society can add a few more. For instance: Wylmeslowe, Willmeslawe, Wilmislawe, Wylmyslow, Willmislowed, Wylmuslowe, Wimmislowe, Wymmeslow, Wymslowe, Wemslow, and Welmeslowe, to name but a few.

Spinning Cottons on and Wives get Weaving

As nothing much happened for several centuries apart from the odd church and stately home being built, we shall take the liberty of leaping forward a few score years to the period when Wilmslow first started to make a bit of a name for itself, albeit in a rather small way. Around 1735, two Macclesfield button manufacturers visited the town and gave work to women and children making mohair and silk buttons. The children, some as young as six, earned four (old) pence a day and their mothers four shillings a week. It wasn't much, but it was the start of industrial activity which was to develop quite rapidly.

This was due mainly to three inventors about whom every Lancashire schoolboy should be able to write a book; Sir Richard Arkwright, James Hargreaves and Samuel Crompton. The spinning jenny and spinning mule enabled inhabitants to set up business in their own homes. The locals in Wilmslow quickly cottoned on to the fact that spinners were in great demand and in no time at all almost every cottage had at least one spinning machine, sometimes three or four. Initially they spun jersey for Yorkshire woollen manufacturers but this was superseded by cotton. The spinners could produce only 1lb (about 0.5kg) of coarse yarn a day and it took 10 of them to keep one weaver busy – hardly adequate. They augmented the output from a handful of mills which appeared around 1780 near the parish church on the banks of the Bollin, using Arkwright's water-powered machine.

Ralph Bower built a mill with a water wheel for carding and became rich enough to buy the Hawthorn estate. Then came Barbers silk mill on the Carrs and Samuel Greg built Quarry Bank Mill in Styal (1784). All this activity gave the standard of living a welcome boost. Villagers had never had it so good. They dumped their clogs and bought shoes; homes were extended to accommodate more jennies, bringing work for joiners and bricklayers; more shops appeared and butchers couldn't get enough meat – some was brought from Yorkshire.

The "aristocrats" of all this were the weavers, a skilled bunch who earned big money out of their handlooms. But the revolution in spinning didn't reach weaving for some time. Weavers, who had not been able to get enough yarn from hand spinners,

4

were able to work at full pace when the powered spinning machines arrived. It is said that some walked about with cash stuffed in their hatbands and their wives drank tea out of best china.

Everybody wanted to get in on the act, and, as always seems to happen in boom times, a few unscrupulous men seized their opportunity. Weaving instructors charged half their earnings for up to two years. No doubt cries of "Rip off" or words to that effect, could be heard frequently in the hostelries.

However, some high-productivity weavers were earning up to £2 a week by 1800. It wasn't only money that was sloshing about – quarts of ale were being supped in alarming quantities.

Henry Greg, who owned the Ship Inn at Styal, was so concerned about drunkenness that he limited customers to two glasses of beer each. And Samuel Finney, J.P., of Fulshaw Hall, declared the "licentiousness and disorders of the lower rank of people intolerable". It is said that he managed to quell the Wilmslow Jersey Combers who then behaved "with much more reserve". Finney also improved roads and made new bridges "so that post-chaises and gentlemen's carriages began to whirl along the roads to the great amazement and pleasure of the gazing country people".

As the standard of living for most people improved, so did the population. By 1787 about 150 were employed in the local mills. More arrived from other parts of the country to work at Styal. They lived at places like Handforth, Morley and Mottram. Mills employed young children drawn from far away, but a law was passed in 1802 restricting the distance they could be transported. Their conditions were hard. Younger apprentices, some aged only 10 or 11, worked 60 or more hours and received only about a shilling a week, although they were housed, clothed and fed.

Two youngsters at Styal reported that their rooms were kept clean and aired and floors washed. They slept two to a bed and were grateful enough to have clean sheets once a month, which must have been cause for celebration. Every two years they had new clothes for Sundays when they attended church. The mill was also responsible for their education and medical care. Despite, or perhaps because of, the strictness of their environment, there was a certain amount of vandalism and truancy. Scrumping a few apples could cost a hefty 5s. (25p) fine. In the early 1800s one third of the labour force at Styal consisted of apprentices. Quarry Bank Mill, with its huge 32ft diameter wheel, prospered for 40 years until it hit a bad patch between 1825-1840 when it lost £15,000.

Power loom weaving was introduced in 1835 and the mill continued to operate until it finally closed on 30th October, 1959. It is now a working museum and popular tourist attraction.

The Boom goes Bust

By 1825 the good times started by Arkwright and Hargreaves were coming to an end. Steam powered looms killed off much of the handloom weaving – a massive blow as a large part of the population of 4,000 were involved in it in some way. There was a slump in trade and women were employed instead of men because they were much cheaper. Those who had been earning £2 thirty years earlier were now picking up only 10 shillings (50p).

One eminent young gentleman who watched the decline with more than a passing interest was a certain William Ewart Gladstone, who was being taught in Wilmslow by the Rector, the Rev J.M. Turner, as a 19-year-old. Gladstone certainly benefited from this education for he went on to become Liberal Prime Minister (having been a Tory) from 1868-74, and again 1880-85, 1886, and 1892-94. Apart from being a classical scholar and writer on church matters he was a strong advocate of liberal causes.

By the time he entered Parliament as a Tory in 1832, Gladstone would certainly have been aware that the halcyon days were over. Even the silk buttons had gone out of fashion to be replaced by metal ones. The silk mill on the Carrs closed and became a laundry. It finally came to an ignominious end when it was destroyed by fire on 4th October, 1923. Wilmslow seems to have escaped the turmoil of the Luddite riots. In Manchester, workers went on the rampage smashing the machines which were putting them out of work.

In 1819 word reached Wilmslow of what became known as the Peterloo massacre. Troops attacked a protesting crowd of workers in Manchester, killing 11 and wounding 400.

Prices had soared because of a depreciated currency. The unemployed paraded the streets demanding food. The poor rate went up from two shillings to five shillings, and income tax went up to two shillings in the pound.

Napoleon wasn't totally to blame, but the little confrontation at Waterloo in 1815 didn't do Britain's economy a lot of good. In the late twenties there was a financial depression and many signs of deprivation. Farmworkers in particular, with their six shillings a week, could not afford much. People had few clothes and some villagers used to walk barefoot to church, carrying their shoes, and then putting them on outside.

A butcher's cart came from Derbyshire each week and sold mutton outside the George and Dragon at four pence a pound. It seemed reasonably cheap, but few could afford it. This was in sharp contrast to the golden days 50 years earlier when demand exceeded supply. Travelling did not present a problem – people walked. They thought nothing of a 15-mile trudge to Macclesfield and back.

Graphic descriptions of the hard times are given in a book with the curious title of *"Wilmslow Graves and Grave Thoughts from Wilmslow"* by Alfred Fryer. Bridget Earnshaw, who had worked in a mill at the age of ten, spoke of a cruel master with a twig-whip, made of plaited twigs. "He beat me if I looked away", she said. She earned two shillings (10p) a week but later got nearly 10 shillings (50p) as a weaver. Benjamin Johnson recalled working in a mill from 6am to 9pm, also as a 10-year-old and earning 1s 6d. a week. He remembered seeing Gladstone, "tall and thin", walking with two dogs. They lived mainly on potatoes, buttermilk and porridge. "Water and filth used to run down the middle of the street and it was very foul, especially in hot weather". In 1833 an attempt was made to improve the lot of children. A Factory Act was passed preventing children under nine from working; those under 13 were limited to nine hours and those aged 13-18 to 12 hours.

However, the poor just couldn't win – most factory owners ignored the Act. It seemed that the only thing a man could do was to drown his sorrows, but even that was a bit of a problem. Beer cost eight pence a quart, (they didn't mess about with pints in those days) and most people couldn't afford it. However, they were determined not to be beaten ... they got together and brewed their own!

Chapter 2: A Simply Wizard Away-Day

Railway trippers enjoy "pure air" and buns

The emergence of urbanised Wilmslow and its neighbours dates back to the arrival of the railway in 1842, five years after Queen Victoria came to the throne. The line from Manchester via Stockport was opened on 10th May by the Manchester and Birmingham Railway, later the London and North Western Railway. (The Styal line was not built until 67 years later.) The first line was soon extended to Alderley

Crowds flocked to see the royal train on its way through Wilmslow on 14th July, 1913. It was carrying King George V and Queen Mary back to London. Railway buffs might like to know that it was pulled by two 4-4-0 George V class locos, " Loyalty" and "St. George".

and free season tickets for 21 years were offered to Manchester businessmen who agreed to build a house with a rateable value of at least £50 within one mile of the stations. The motive for this unusual act of generosity is unclear, but it would appear to have been a means of creating a commuter town, thus ensuring fare revenue.

Judging by some of the comments written about Manchester at the time there must have been quite a rush. One peer described it as "a great nasty manu-facturing town". General Sir Charles Napier said: "Hell may be paved with good intentions but it is hung with Manchester cottons". Another literary gent said it was "a foul drain and filthy sewer... inhabitants work in half daylight because black smoke always obscures the sun".

These, of course, were comments of aristocrats who didn't like the look of the new world of industry and commerce. This non-aristocratic writer worked in Manchester for 30 years (not in the 1800s) and also

The arrival of the railway brought new life to Wilmslow. This picture of the station, which opened on 10th May, 1842, was taken about 90 years ago. There is an advertising hoarding over the entrance for Charles Charnley's pharmacy, which stills exists in Grove Street. On the left is Lord Vernon's coal depot for Poynton and Worth Collieries. In 1894 the urban council complained in a letter to the Advertiser about the disgraceful condition of the station and said it failed to measure up to the status of the town. In more recent times, until the station finally got a face-lift to match its smart new surroundings, there were many who believed that a similar complaint would not have been out of place.

The attractive-looking Railway Hotel on Station Road was built not many years after the railway opened and was a popular overnight stop for passengers. Several years later, the front garden had to go for road widening . . . now, sadly, the hotel has gone too (see Chapter 7).

regarded it as a depressing place, full of Lowry-type characters seemingly resigned to a grim way of life, but not quite as bad a place as described by the other more eminent characters. Perhaps the secretary of the Manchester Literary Club summed it up adequately when he described Manchester as "a capital place to get away from".

Alderley became a favourite spot for day-trippers enjoying an away-day from Manchester. Louisa Stanley, eldest daughter of the first Lord Stanley of Alderley, wrote of the pleasure of a party of Sunday School teachers and scholars "in seeing such scenery and breathing such pure air". Maria, Lady Stanley described the arrival of between 2,000 and 3,000 trippers one day. "Sundry fields were hired from the farmers to eat buns and to play about in, the buns having been part of a special train allotted to them". A train returning to Manchester in June, 1843, had trippers crammed into 63 coaches, many of which were uncovered.

The Wizard inn, formerly the Miners Arms and now a restaurant, entertained trippers with rifle shooting, archery, coconut shies, donkey rides, dancing and swing boats. Strangely, the LNWR charged full fare for children and no luggage was allowed. A poster dated 1863 advertises "cheap trips" on Saturdays during the season leaving Manchester London Road at 2.15 p.m. calling at Stockport and Wilmslow and returning from Alderley at 9 p.m. Return fares were two shillings or one shilling according to class. The fare cost the same from either Manchester or Stockport.

Those who preferred a trip to the seaside could take "a sea-bathing special for the working classes" from Manchester to Fleetwood and Blackpool. Fares were 3 shillings (15p) for men and – surprisingly generously – half price not only for children but women, too. The railways guaranteed that travellers would be able to "bathe and refresh themselves in ample time to attend a place of worship". How times change.

A poster for the 1891 Alderley Wakes: so easy to get to on the LNWR, though Farm Labourers entering the 150yds Scratch Race would, presumably, have walked there.

LONDON & NORTH WESTERN RAILWAY.

CHEAP TRIPS,

On Saturday Afternoons,

TO ALDERLEY.

Every Saturday during the Season, a

SPECIAL TRAIN

will leave the

LONDON ROAD STATION, MANCHESTER, AT 2-15 P.M.,

And STOCKPORT, at 2-30 p.m.,

For ALDERLEY, returning from ALDERLEY at Nine p.m., and calling in going and returning at WILMSLOW.

FARES TO ALDERLEY AND BACK,

From MANCHESTER or STOCKPORT,

1st Class 2s.   Covered Carriages 1s.

Children Full Fare.

NO LUGGAGE ALLOWED

By order.

W. CAWKWELL,

General Manager.

Euston Station, London, July, 1863.

A poster of July, 1863, offering cheap trips to Alderley from Manchester. It wasn't cheap for the children – they had to pay full fare.

LANCASHIRE & YORKSHIRE RAILWAY.

SEA BATHING

FOR THE

WORKING CLASSES.

ON AND AFTER SUNDAY MORNING NEXT, and on each succeeding Sunday until further notice, with a view of affording the benefit of

SEA BATHING,

A Train will leave the following Stations for

FLEETWOOD AND BLACKPOOL.

	FARES THERE AND BACK THE SAME DAY.		
	A.M.	Males.	Females & Children.
Leave Manchester at	6 0	3s. 0d.	1s. 6d.
„ Bolton at	6 30	2s. 0d.	1s. 3d.
„ Chorley at	7 10	2s. 0d.	1s. 0d.
„ Preston at	7 40	2s. 0d.	1s. 0d.

Arriving at Fleetwood at 9 a.m.

FROM SALFORD STATION.

MANCHESTER TO LIVERPOOL

FARES there and back same day.

		Males.	Females and Children.
At 7 a.m.		2s. 6d.	1s. 6d.

BURY TO LIVERPOOL, BLACKPOOL, AND FLEETWOOD.

FARES there and back same day.

		Males.	Females and Children.
At 6 20 a.m.		2s. 6d.	1s. 6d.

Parties availing themselves of these trains will be enabled to

BATHE & REFRESH THEMSELVES

In ample time to attend a Place of Worship.

These Trains will return punctually at 6 p.m., arriving at Manchester about 8 and o'clock

The Tickets will take the Passengers to the above-named places for ONE FARE, but for the purpose of preventing any unnecessary confusion or BUSINESS ON THE SUNDAY, it is desirable that tickets be taken on SATURDAY EVENING.

The working classes who preferred the seaside to the countryside could take a three shillings day trip to Blackpool or Fleetwood. This poster advised that travellers would be able to "bathe and refresh themselves" with ample time to attend church. Note that the journey from Manchester took three hours.

Chapter 3: 'Derby Day' at Lindow — Wakes Week and Fun at the Races

Anyone driving from Altrincham Road to the Newgate refuse tip will probably be puzzled by the name of the approach road, Racecourse Road. Did Wilmslow really have racing? Yes, most certainly. They were held for about 70 years from 1810 to 1880 and Lindow Common must have looked a bit like a miniature Epsom Downs on Derby Day. The three-day meetings were held in Wakes Week, starting on the first Sunday after 28th August. There was a wooden grandstand on the west side of the common and the event caused considerable upheaval. The races were said to be "of inferior character, causing much harm to the neighbourhood".

There was a "purse" of £50 for the best of three, three-mile heats, three times round the course. Racing began "precisely at four o'clock". Those who didn't care much for the gallops had an amazing array of alternative attractions. A handbill announced that there would be "assemblies, cookings and ordinaries as usual".

It is not clear what "ordinaries" were, but they may have had something to do with the following events: "wheelbarrow and pig races, quoiting, cricket, wrestling, dipping, whistling, humming, soaking, knitting, bobbing, poling, dancing, singing, snuff-taking and pudding-eating". What type of pudding is not mentioned – black pudding, perhaps? Humming conjures up an interesting scene, and the snuff-taking was no doubt a contest not to be sneezed at.

Poling probably referred to the art of climbing greased poles to reach a leg of mutton at the top. This would be a particularly treasured prize as the local farm workers and weavers earned only around 10 shillings (50p) a week and never saw meat on their table except in Wakes Week which was the big occasion of the year. Apart from the events at the races, the town itself celebrated in style too. People didn't go away to Blackpool, and why should they? There was far more fun in Church Street than on the promenade. It was a time of family gatherings and feastings.

A contemporary diarist called Cedric, writing in Cheshire Notes and Queries, describes the jollifications. Each pub had a fiddler and a board was put on the taproom floor for a form of tap dancing. (No, this is not how taprooms came to be so-called.) In addition to the aforementioned "ordinaries" there were fire-eaters, conjurers, card-sharpers, dog fights, bull and bear baiting.

These Wakes Week celebrations were the forerunner of to-day's carnivals. The first of its kind was held in 1909 and raised money for a horse ambulance. Church Street was lined with stalls and there was a

All dressed up for the carnival about 1912. The owner is Robert Bourne, a grocer. He also built houses in Bourne Street, which was named after him. The first carnival was held in 1909 and superseded the Wakes Week celebrations of the 1800s.

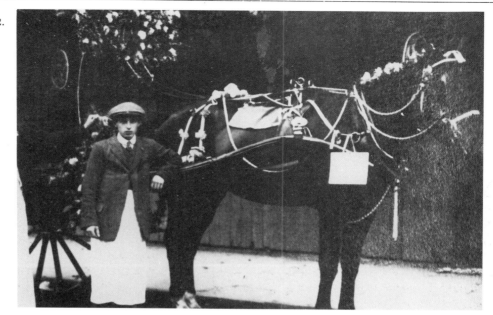

The firemen's turnout is among the leaders as the 1912 carnival procession winds its way around the Wilmslow streets, watched by hundreds of enthusiastic townsfolk.

Morris dancers at the Wilmslow Carnival

long procession through the town of tradesmen's "turnouts" and other decorated floats, led by a band. Some of the carts contained bakers actually baking bread and blacksmiths working at their anvil. In the evening there was a torchlight procession, with the carts lit by candles and torches, followed by fireworks and a bonfire in a field near the New Inn. It can be safely assumed that a right good time was had by all.

Mists and Mystique

The racecourse was just one of many fascinating aspects of Lindow. Even without the exciting discovery of the unfortunate Pete, Lindow Moss and Common, with its Black Lake and heavy mists, has undoubtedly a romantic mystique about it. Lindow once stretched from the Kings Arms on Knutsford Road, believed to have been built as the Fulshaw

Even regulars at the King's Arms may well have difficulty recognising their old hostelry in this 1910 scene at Fulshaw Cross. The pub, just to the right of centre in the picture, has, of course, been rebuilt, but the cottage on the left is still there.

The same scene at Fulshaw Cross today, just recognisable by the white cottage on the left.

The Fulshaw Cross, now re-sited alongside the Knutsford Road roundabout. Crosses were introduced about the 7th century by missionaries who held religious services around them. See also page 19.

Cross about 1830, to Hawthorn Lane. It originally covered 1500 acres, but is now only about 150 acres. It wasn't unheard of for men and cattle to be lost in its treacherous bog.

Many of its inhabitants at one time were Gypsies, mainly tinkers, who hawked clothes pegs and who were said to bake hedgehogs in clay. The common also had Lindow gnats which were noted for their appetite, and another nasty pet – vipers. They were so numerous that a viper-catcher was called in once a year to deal with them. They were about a foot long and highly poisonous – a pointer dog bitten by one died within 12 hours.

In the 18th century most inhabitants lived precariously off the land, grazing their cows, sheep and geese on the common. Later, many of them went over to weaving. Those who fell upon hard times when tenancies were abruptly taken away, were forced to live in the workhouse which stood on the site of the present Gorsey Bank School. One of its residents was old Billy Cash, the village bellman.

He used to stroll along the streets ringing his bell and attracting attention with the traditional shouts of "Oyez". Apart from making official announcements he also did a few commercials, "broadcasting" private messages such as a brooch being lost. Apart from having a good business sense he apparently had a good sense of humour, too, for he usually ended his oration by declaring: "God bless the Queen and me".

There is a splendid tale handed down over the years of a man named Percival, who lived in Lindow in 1820. Apparently he was a bit of a lad, often drunk, and nicknamed Modesty for reasons which are unclear. Going home the worse for wear one night, he fell into a geese watering hole and drowned.

The locals prepared this amusing epitaph for his grave:

Who lies here?
Who do you think?
Poor old Modesty,
Bring him some drink
Bring him some drink
I tell you for why
When he was living
He was always dry.

The superstitious villagers, however, were afraid to joke about Modesty in case his ghost appeared and the epitaph was never used.

Another lane in the Fulshaw area which has changed quite a lot since 1900 but is still recognised without too much trouble is Hawthorn Street, shown here looking towards Altrincham Road. The cottages on the left have gone.

The grim-looking workhouse was built on Altrincham Road, Lindow, about 1772, on the present site of Gorsey Bank School. Not much is known about it, although it is thought to have existed for some 60 or 70 years and eventually became a farmhouse. Many workhouses were set up under private Acts for the relief of the aged, orphans and the sick.

A picturesque scene at Lindow Common as skaters take advantage of an icy day many years ago when the Black Lake turned a wintry white.

Fire and Plague Sweep the Common

By 1836 the Lindow population had reached 193, of whom, it is recorded, 101 were Methodists, two Baptists, one Independent, 10 who went to church, and 79 who didn't. The Friends Meeting House built by the Quakers on Altrincham Road was one of the earliest places of worship. Now, sadly, like many other old buildings in the area, it has been converted into offices.

Two big fires swept the heath, one in 1852 and one in May, 1865, which "burned for several weeks with great fury". Pete, resting several feet down, was not unduly concerned with such matters, nor with a plague which swept the area in 1866, killing 19 children. The peat, which today is cut and sent off to mushroom farms, was once burned to supply heat for cottages.

It is found below the first layer of turf and is cut to a depth of five feet. The inventive villagers also cut fir trees into thin strips which were used as a substitute for candles. Old fossilised fir trees have been found in the spongy ground which oozes ankle-deep

A 1930s view of the Fulshaw cross area before the cross, which stood at the corner of Bedells Lane, was moved to make way for the roundabout, from where the brave or foolhardy can picture the scene. The shop, now a hair salon, was a greengrocer's.

mud. Lindow shared in the general population growth of Wilmslow and by 1870 it had nearly 500 inhabitants. On 22nd June, 1897, John Royle handed over the racecourse land to the public to mark Queen Victoria's diamond jubilee.

Amazingly, during the early 1980s, in this aquatic climate of ours the shallow Black Lake sprang a leak and dried up. Water seeped out through the bed into the sand below, leaving an ugly sea of mud. The lake has now been excavated and the problem solved by lining it with a layer of mineral clay.

The common, with its unique habitat, is a rare lowland heath below 1,000 feet. It is designated as a Site of Special Scientific Interest and is managed by the borough council in conjunction with the Nature Conservancy Council. The common has a part-time ranger, plus volunteers, who, among other duties, keep unwanted visitors like motor-cyclists away; much less harmful visitors like model boat enthusiasts and anglers are also discouraged. Parties of schoolchildren use it for nature study – there is said to be a wealth of flora and fauna and over 100 bird species have been spotted there.

Chapter 4: The Golden Square Mile

Nice Shops – Pity about the Dungeon and Toll Bar

With the popularity of the railway and the influence of Manchester, Wilmslow's population had risen to about 5,000 by 1850, an increase of 50 per cent over 50 years, and a large proportion of the villagers were concentrated in a small area centred on Church Street. Clustered around the church were sundry higgledy-piggledy cottages, like cygnets snuggling up to a protective mother swan. This was where it all happened, a sort of Golden Square Mile.

Church Street itself had three pubs, the George and Dragon, the Ring o'Bells and the Vine. There had been a fourth pub, the Bull's Head, but it is uncertain how long it lasted. There were at least 20 shops, their owners living either above or alongside their premises. They included Griffiths the hairdresser, Ogden's clog shop, Chandler's cooked foods, Ollerenshaw the butcher's, and Antrobus's sweet shop (mint and lemon humbugs eight for a penny.) The market didn't arrive until after the last war.

About 70 families lived there, most people working in agriculture and cotton, or as servants. There was the village pump (which somehow came to be moved to Mobberley at a later date), a convalescent home – and the infamous dungeon. This was on Dungeon Walk, the passageway which runs from Church Street past Burton House to the rear of the Post Office.

It was built in 1809, about the time the stocks were abolished, and contained two cells in which prisoners were left in total darkness. One commentator described it as "a loathsome place only fit for newts, toads and other vermin". Villagers were no doubt highly delighted when it was demolished about 1860.

A regular "guest" in the dungeon was a tearaway called "Old Jeppy" who had a distinct liking for a drop of alcohol. His guards were not averse to the odd bribe which Jeppy managed to slip to them through an iron grill over the door. They then nipped along to the nearby Ring o' Bells to buy a noggin of gin which was ingeniously drip-fed to Jeppy through a clay pipe inserted through the keyhole.

There was also the gas works which William Bower built in 1846 to supply his mill. As the use of gas became more popular, the works became the Wilmslow and Alderley Edge Gas Company. An explosion here on August 5, 1871 killed six men, one of whom was deputising for a workmate. Before the turnpike arrived along Manchester Road and Grove Street, coaches used Lacey Green, Cliff Road, Church Street and Green Lane. Although sewage was disposed of through open ditches and channels, at least one gentleman was concerned with the environment.

A mill-owner ordered the chimney of his factory to be knocked down to help keep Wilmslow residen-

Despite the many changes, Church Street, probably the most historic in the town, is easily recognisable from this view. The old Ring o' Bells pub is halfway up the street on the right, and the little shop bottom left is Cooper's the grocers.

The Safeways supermarket, halfway up on the left, now dominates Church Street. Now that additional redevelopment has taken place, including a new block of apartments on the right, just above the George and Dragon, little of the original street remains.

21

Among the many old shops in Church Street was Antrobus's sweet shop. This was next to the Vine Inn, just above the present site of Safeways.

This line of homes on Chancel Lane illustrates how the parish church was once surrounded by tiny cottages. They have long since been demolished.

This picture of the bottom of Church Street shows just how close the cottages on the right were to the church. The cobbled lane below the horse and cart is only a few feet wide. The cottage opposite the church is Sumner's boot and shoe makers.

The George and Dragon has hardly changed, but the pretty, thatched cottages which used to be next door have now been replaced by the pub car park.

23

A closer look at Sumner the boot makers. Some historians have suggested that it might have been a rectory originally, although there is no conclusive evidence of this. A mill chimney can be seen in the background, to the left.

tial. It would be nice to think there was a similar, civic-minded action man around today to restore some aesthetic values. After years of neglect, Church Street has finally lost its tatty hotchpotch of old, derelict eyesores, as redevelopment has taken place.

Grove Street, which had been turnpiked in 1775, was something of a backwater in the early 1800s. Although it was now the main road through Wilmslow (called New Road) it had only five shops including a corn merchant, a wheelwright and a saddler. Without doubt the main cause of the street's unpopularity was the toll bar at the top of the road at the junction with Water Lane.

The charge was three pence a wheel (one shilling a carriage) which makes today's *peages* on the French autoroutes seem like the bargain of a lifetime. No

wonder coaches to London were so expensive. They had to negotiate several toll bars, including local ones at the Waggon and Horses, Handforth, the De Trafford Hotel, Alderley, the White Lion in Withington, and another in Cheadle.

The fare was about £3 sitting inside and £2 in the fresh air section. The journey usually took about four days, but one driver knew how to 'step on the horses'. William Watmough did the trip around 1840 in his express, four-in-hand coach "Lady Nelson" in 17 hours, an average speed of 11 mph, including stops. What the passengers thought about it is not recorded. Regular halts were made at places like the Grove Inn in Grove Street, which was situated on or near the present Halifax Building Society building.

The Grove had a bowling green, orchard and gar-

den, much more agreeable for the passengers of yester-year than some of today's unappealing motorway cafes. The Grove existed up to about 1840, then became a private house of the Bowers. It was converted into shops in the late 1880s. The toll bar, erected about 1805 after being moved from Brook Lane, Alderley Edge, was a continuous source of resentment.

It was run by the Highway Board, "a band of puppets who spend an hour a month with their legs under the table in the board room of the Union workhouse at Macclesfield". Wilmslow people, it was said, were "taxed to maintain in repair, roads around Macclesfield which they seldom or never use". Eventually the toll bar was removed with jubilant and excited crowds leaping about like fans welcoming home Manchester United with the Cup. It was scheduled for removal on 1st January, 1877, but the townsfolk couldn't wait.

Angry tradesmen planned to smash the toll bar with axes during a midnight procession on New Year's Eve, followed by fireworks and effigy burning. However, their courage didn't live up to their bravado and they abandoned the plan. The next morning, workmen of Sir Humphrey de Trafford arrived to dismantle the gate. Just to make sure everyone was completely satisfied, ale was doled out to the multitude, who gave three cheers for "deliverance from the bars".

It is hard to imagine Grove Street once looking like this. The picture shows the toll bar which infuriated townsfolk for about 70 years until it was demolished in 1877 amid scenes of great jubilation. Carriages had to pay a toll of three pence per wheel.

This was busy, bustling Grove Street with two-way traffic. The shop on the right is J.E. Johnson, described as a motor and cycle dealer, but there does not seem to be much evidence of motors about.

This was the Bank Square area in the early 1900s. Judging by the number of children in the picture, it was taken during the school holidays. The shop on the left is Watson's the confectioners and in the centre is W.S. Clegg's, a former well-known drapers who were in business there for 120 years from 1856. The building on the right with the clock is the Union Bank.

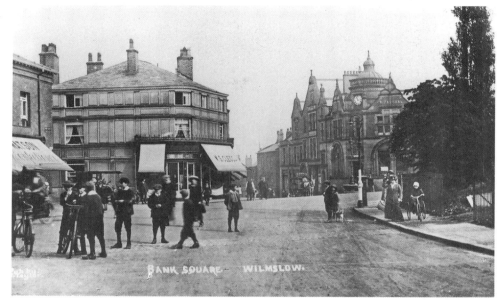

The old toll has gone, but up until mid-1995, there was a toll on the nerves as shoppers jostled each other on the inadequate pavements and drivers tried to squeeze into impossible parking spaces.

27

At last, sanity prevails as Grove Street becomes traffic-free and shopping becomes a pleasure.

Cars no longer drive down Grove Street – only cyclists and skateboards remain as potential hazards.

The Conservative Club on the corner of Grove Street and Grove Avenue was enthusiastically decorated for the coronation of King George V in 1910. Since redevelopment, the site has had a number of different shops.

Still going strong after nearly 130 years, Charnley's the chemists is the last remaining shop of the original "founder members" of Grove Street.

This attractive, leafy road is Grove Avenue, with Hawthorn Hall clearly visible at the end.

Grove Avenue today, still pleasantly leafy despite the addition of many new houses.

A sign behind the old single-decker bus says "Through traffic south", showing that Green Lane was once the main road. Note the trees up the left hand side of Grove Street, which was open to two-way traffic – what little there was. The premises behind the bus was Pickford's, fruit and flower shop.

Look, no traffic! Now, it's pedestrians only in Grove Street, yet the scene has not changed dramatically. The oddly-shaped building on the left at the bottom of the street looks very similar.

The buildings on the right are no longer there, but it is still easy to recognise Manchester Road, looking down the hill from the traffic lights at the Station Road junction. Among the premises was Harveys the saddlers and a cafe.

Fortunately, these disused buildings in Swan Street, which remained an eyesore for far too long, have now been replaced with shops and offices.

The Police Station, Swan Street, on the site of what was Lloyds Bank

As Wilmslow grew, so did the need to accommodate more villains so this new police station was opened in Green Lane. This in turn was closed and reopened as a public house with the not-very-imaginative name of The Blue Lamp. Perhaps Old Nick would have been better. The new, purpose-built police station is in Hawthorn Street.

This is how Station Road and Swan Street looked until the 1930s when the shops on the left were knocked down to make way for what became known as the by-pass. This was the continuation of Manchester Road, seen on the right. The shop on the left is an umbrella repairers.

These quaint thatched cottages on Mill Street were just a few of the dozens clustered around the parish church. The disused mill on the right of the picture may have been the building converted into a lodging house which was nicknamed "the Paddy Can" because it usually contained Irish farm workers.

Sweet Times for 'Quality Street'

Grove Street started to prosper. It acquired the British Workman Hall, a post office and a smithy which made a set of horseshoes for £1. During the last war it made anchors. Today's newly-refurbished arcade was then a tree-lined alley. More family-run shops opened. Only one of them still remains – Charnley's the chemists, which dates back to 1868. Cleggs' the drapers opened in 1856 and served customers for 120 years. Others existed for decades, earning it a "Quality Street" reputation.

They included Clement Owen's wine shop which celebrated its centenary in 1968; it subsequently became another wine shop but this also eventually closed. There was Poole's, which was famous for home-made humbugs, and Berry's the outfitters. Some may find today's multiples and chain stores much more appealing, but there will be many who mourn the passing of the old family businesses. Personally I think they should be a protected species. Other nearby roads in the Golden Mile were starting to move with the times, too.

Swan Street was a bit up market. It boasted a doctor's surgery on the site that is now gardens, a pharmacist, a butcher's and a police station which later became a bank. A passageway lead down the side of the bank to a slaughterhouse. On the corner nearby, on the site of today's Midland Bank, there had been a dry pub run by a temperance society. An inscription outside read:

A public house, without the drink,
Where men may meet, read, talk and think.

There was also, of course, yet another distinctly wet pub, the Swan, an old coaching inn dating back to the early 1800s. It had many stables and ostlers who greeted the mail coach from Manchester which stopped there at noon. In 1880 it was definitely the smart place to stay, boasting that "commercial gentlemen will meet with every comfort".

These included a croquet lawn, Bass's pale ale and other Burton ales and a first class billiard table. The inn also had "broughams, wagonettes, drags, barouches, open and closed carriages of every description always on hire. Weddings and picnic parties attended with four-horse omnibuses". In 1800 the landlord was one Francis Cutts, who also managed to find time to serve as the postmaster.

The public hall, next to the inn, also doubled up as a picture house. It was destroyed by fire in 1920 when it was being used as a shirt factory. Someone thoughtfully put up a drinking fountain outside, but with all those pubs about, it must have been mainly for the benefit of the horses.

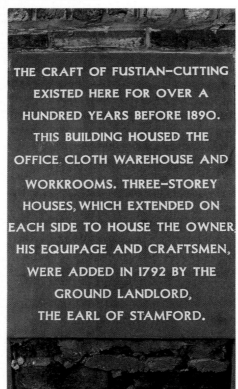

This commemorative plaque, marking the site of a fustian cutting factory, stands by the roadside at Stamford Court, Manchester Road, on the hill near the traffic lights.

This quiet, peaceful road, c.1925, is hardly recognisable as Alderley Road, opposite Hoopers' (formerly Finnigans). The large, gabled house and the one next to it still exist today. The gardens on the left are the grounds of Green Hall.

The familiar heavy traffic now dominates Alderley Road. The two buildings referred to in the old picture can be clearly picked out.

The Towering Twins, 70 Years Apart

Manchester Road, originally the site of an Anglo-Saxon settlement, was another well populated place. There was the obligatory pub, the King's Head, (now renamed the King William) and a busy fustian cutting factory. Fustian was a hard wearing material, like corduroy. Its appearance was improved by cutting loops of the weft. It was a tough job, but welcomed as handloom weaving was on the decline. This factory is now marked by a plaque which can be seen on the roadside at Stamford Court below the row of handsome Georgian houses. About 200 yards away there was another fustian works at the corner of Bollin Walk and Ladyfield Street.

Step across the road and you will see what I believe is one of the most impressive sights in Wilmslow, the twin railway viaducts. They stand there grandly, imperiously, but I wonder how many thousands of people regularly travel over them without realising there are in fact two viaducts side by side. The first was built when the original line to Stockport was opened in 1842. Bollin Hall, which stood at the southern end of the viaducts, was demolished to make way for the railway. Thus, Wilmslow lost a little bit of history, for Anne Boleyn, luckless second wife of Henry VIII, is reputed to have been born there. About 70 years later it was decided a second viaduct was needed when the Styal line opened.

Mill Street, with its pretty, thatched cottages, opposite the church, lost its mill about 1840 when the cotton spinning industry declined. It was bought by an enterprising rag and bone man, an Italian rejoicing in the name of Cornelius Sherriffe, who owned a second hand clothing shop just round the corner in Church Street. He stepped in and converted the mill into a lodging house, charging four pence a night. It housed Irish labourers who worked mainly on the land and the locals nicknamed it the Paddy Can.

The impressive twin viaducts, with their 11 arches, were built 70 years apart. The first was built for the Stockport line which opened in 1842. Bollin Hall, reputed to be the birthplace of Anne Boleyn, was demolished to make way for it.

Across the road was a Methodist mission. This, along with a row of a dozen weavers' cottages opposite the church on Chancel Lane, disappeared when it was decided to widen the road. They were replaced by the attractive memorial gardens. More cottages were demolished in 1862 when the River Bollin was diverted away from the church. Chancel Lane school was built on the site of the current Carrs car park in

Another road that has changed so much that it is hardly recognisable is Water Lane. The three gentlemen standing outside J. & N. Mills stonemason's yard at the junction with Grove Street, could not have guessed that it would become such a frantically busy corner.

Water Lane today. The half timbered building on the left, occupied by Thomas Cook's, is the same one seen in the old picture.

Looking down Water Lane towards Altrincham. Note that the properties on the right were all houses, not shops, in those days. Kennerleys Lane is on the right.

This was how Green Lane looked before the whole area was redeveloped. The garage was approximately where the arcade is today.

1868 for "children of poorer classes" and had 350 pupils.

Green Lane (formerly Old Road), also had several cottages and a smithy. It was the main road until the turnpike was built up Grove Street. Now, there is not much there apart from the Blue Lamp which was formerly the police station, the Roman Catholic church, and back entrances to shops. But this small part of the town centre was at one time virtually a hamlet in its own right.

Parsonage Green, one of several greens like Morley and Lacey, was not much more than a row of cottages facing the Rectory. Early inhabitants watched in horror as Cromwells's men besieged the original rectory in the 17th century civil war. The rector, the Rev. Thomas Wright, was captured.

Residents of the 20th century may also have watched in horror in the 1930s as the Green disappeared to make way for a by-pass. Today, as another generation of planners celebrates the completion of a new by-pass to by-pass the old by-pass, the Green is a prosperous mixture of shops and businesses. Another bit of the area's history to disappear in heated fashion, and somewhat more abruptly, was the council offices, now the site of a Romany caravan. They went up in flames in 1978, but as the council itself had been engulfed by Macclesfield six years earlier, it wasn't regarded as too much of a blow. The

council started life in 1875 as the Wilmslow Local Board and became the U.D.C. in 1894.

However, many were sad that Wilmslow had lost such a fine building. Green Hall, described as "one of the most cosy mansions in the parish", was formerly a private residence standing in its own large grounds. It belonged to the Paulden family, who owned a large department store in Manchester. (Hands up all those who admit being old enough to remember Pauldens before it become Debenhams).

This is a quaint and unusual little bit of history of which Wilmslow can be justly proud – the Romany Caravan. It was used for holidays by the family of the Rev George Bramwell Evens, a Methodist minister, who became famous through his Children's Hour broadcasts on the wireless during the last war. Known to millions as "Romany", he gave fascinating talks on natural history. He retired to Wilmslow in 1939 and died in November 1943. The caravan, which was acquired by the Evenses in 1921, was subsequently given to the then Wilmslow Urban District Council. It was restored and is now in the hands of Macclesfield Council, who open it to the public on specific dates each year. It is next to the public library, in peaceful and tranquil memorial gardens ideal for a quiet spot of meditation, just a stone's throw from the town's noisy traffic.

Any resident recognising this road gets full marks. It is Styal Road, looking towards Manchester Road in the distance. Cliff Road is on the right.

Mature trees now obscure the houses along Styal Road today.

Chapter 5: Alarming Days at the Fire Station

Calling out firemen to a blaze at the turn of the last century must have been a bit like a scene from a Keystone Cops film. I wonder what a fire officer of today would make of this urban council bye-law of 1897: "The officer in charge shall furnish his men with the necessary refreshments at a fire, the cost to be defrayed by the local board". If the urgency of the turn-out was anything to go by, the officer would have had time to wander off and find a Chinese takeaway.

A fire alarm was sounded by the "steam roarer" at the gasworks and every member of the brigade had to proceed to the engine house. The first man was to get the engine ready. The second was to go to the gasworks to find out where the fire was, plus the name and address of the informant, then return "and write down the particulars on the board provided".

It was then "at the discretion of the captain or officer in command to turn out or otherwise". The dashing about was not too much of a problem from the original station which was nearby in Green Lane, but some fine sprinters must have been required when the station was moved to Hawthorn Street in 1909. The installation of a telephone three years later no doubt brought big sighs of relief. The present premises in Altrincham Road were opened on 5th June, 1964.

In the earlier days, before the arrival of a motorised fire engine (with solid tyres) in the early 1920s, there was also the slight problem of making sure there were a couple of horses available to pull the engine. Fire-duty horses were also used to pull cabs, so if a fare was unfortunate enough to be half-way to his destination when the "steam roarer" sounded, he was politely told to bale out, the horses unhitched, taken back to the station and then hitched to the engine. By the time the firemen finally arrived, the blaze was no doubt burning merrily.

An ordinary fireman was paid 10 shillings a week. The cost of calling out the fire brigade must have been a considerable deterrent. These were the call-out charges within the district – it was even dearer outside:

Engine: 21 shillings; two horses 21s.
Services per fireman: 2s. for first hour, 1s, for every subsequent hour.
Helpers and pumpers: six pence per hour.
Cleaning engine: six pence per hour.

Fortunately, victims were not required to pay for firemen's refreshments, too. When the public hall in Swan Street burned down on 7th December, 1921, the total fire bill was £35. The bill for the Carrs Mill fire two years later was £33. In the case of smaller fires, it must have been a big temptation to tell the firemen to go to blazes!

Ready for action, the Wilmslow firemen of about 1910. Their horses were also used to draw cabs and had to be unhitched and galloped back to the station if the "steam roarer" alarm sounded at the gas works.

Spick and span and ready for instant action – that's the Wilmslow fire crew of more modern times.

Tactful Tips for Cabbies

Cabbies, too, had to conform to the strict regulations laid down in the bye-laws of 1880. The authorities were quite firm on who should, or should not be transported. For instance they were dead against corpses. A cabbie should not "knowingly convey the dead body of any person", and if he did find a deceased, he had to notify the Inspector of Nuisances. (It would be a bit of a nuisance, having a body in the back).

A hackney carriage could be drawn by horse, pony, mule, ass or goat and there was to be no excessive galloping. The speed limit was 4 m.p.h. Anyone who has endured a taxi driver looking on with indifference as you struggle with your luggage, would appreciate a law which required a cabbie to "offer all reasonable assistance in removing baggage to or from any door or entrance".

The authorities were quite conscious of their social and environmental responsibilities, too. Cabbies were not allowed to ply for hire before 7 a.m. or after midnight. They were also not allowed to smoke (anti-smokers might consider it worth an inquiry to see if this law still applies.) A driver had a good incentive to be honest. He was obliged to return lost goods to their owner, assuming the owner could be found, but was entitled to demand 5 per cent of their value, up to a maximum of £2.

The distance a carriage could travel was also strictly regulated, according to the type of animal doing the hauling. For a horse, pony or mule the maximum was five miles; for an ass three miles; for a goat or goats two miles. A cab hand-drawn by a man had, significantly, the same limit as an ass.

Curiously, a driver could charge by distance or time, although there were no indications as to which method was to be chosen. For two horses it was 4s. an hour or 1s. 6d. a mile; for a pony the respective charges were 2s. and 9d; and for goats 6d. and 6d., but they were only allowed to carry up to two children and no adults. It would not require a degree in mathematics to work out that it was more economical to pay by the mile.

Hotels Keep a Clean Sheet

If rules and regulations were tough for cabbies, they were even worse for lodging-house keepers. The bye-laws stipulated that all floors had to be swept each day before 10 a.m. and washed once a week. And it was reassuring to know that bedclothes and bedding, plus the seat, walls and floor of the privy, had to be "thoroughly cleaned from time to time". Bedding also had to be exposed to the air for one hour, morning and afternoon, after a room had been vacated.

Bedroom windows had to be left open for an hour each a.m. and p.m., except if a person was ill in bed or if the weather was very bad. And to make sure there was no hanky-panky, a male over 10 was not allowed to occupy the bedroom of a female. Presumably this law was not applicable to married couples.

Chapter 6: A Boom in Churches

And St Bart's Staggers on from Century to Century

It's a fairly safe bet that if you ask someone the way to, say, The Carrs, they will direct you past a Burger Shop, and left at the pub then right at the bank. Even if they are on the route, you are unlikely to hear anyone tell you to go to past the chapel or turn left at the church, which would have been the case a century ago when there was something of a boom in church and chapel building. Curiously, they are the biggest edifices and yet the least noticed. Perhaps the church authorities should consider putting up neon signs outside.

The exception, of course, is St Bartholomew's Parish Church, built about the 13th century by the Fittons of Bollin Hall. The first rector was Roger Phyton (Fitton) circa 1250. The church appears to have survived over the years mainly thanks to periodical patching up and the worthy parishioners dipping hands generously into pockets. It was first rebuilt early in the 16th century.

In the 1600s, families installed their own pews of all shapes and sizes making the aisles "ludicrous, like a child's puzzle". The width of the centre aisle varied from 7ft to 3ft. While there was a considerable amount of money spent on things like pews, the wealthier parishioners had a strangely ambivalent attitude towards the poor. They were happy to subscribe money and food, yet were far less charitable when it came to church matters. Only one pew was set aside for the poor and that was in the coldest and most remote part of the church.

By 1835 the building was in a poor state again. The floor was so bad that a box had to be brought for the minister to stand on if the weather was bad. It is reported that "the flooring of the pews generally was so rotten that a careless footstep would have plunged into the coffins of the dead, which were in several instances within a few inches of the bottom of the pews".

In 1862 more repairs were desperately needed and a comprehensive restoration costing £4,000 was carried out. Part of the River Bollin was diverted to extend the churchyard and about a dozen thatched cottages were demolished. What the long-suffering poor thought about this is not recorded, but it may well have lead to a significant change in their church-going habits.

The porch was found to be unsafe and was rebuilt (£300) with every stone being numbered and replaced in the same place. The belfry stage was rebuilt in 1872 (another £700) and the ring of six bells was rehung 16 years later. The oldest is the small bell dated 1657. The others were made about 75 years later. There is an apocryphal story that the bells once rang themselves. This is simply explained by the fact that all six bell-ringers were named Bell. I suspect this tale originated in an olde worlde Christmas cracker.

45

The untidy cluster of weavers' cottages in Chancel Lane have long since gone, to be replaced by the memorial gardens and this peaceful view of St. Bartholomew's Church.

The parish church in Wilmslow tried an experiment in pigeon keeping in 1670. A door was installed at the top of the steeple to prevent "fowleinge" but it didn't work. Then they tried using a net for a few years and that, too, proved useless. Eventually patience ran out and in 1688 it was decided to "expend two pence on powder and shotte". End of problem. And pigeons.

Further restoration took place in 1897. The graveyard has some very old slabs, including a rare one from 1596. An aged sundial is, like the church, designated a listed building. (The church, grade 1, the sundial, grade 2). Inside, there are a large number of monuments and tablets to the Finney, Brownlow, Davenport, Newton, Booth, Roylance and Trafford families.

The most remarkable historical record, however, is the parish register which dates from 1558. The churchwardens' accounts are reasonably well preserved and specify in great detail, expenditure and receipts. They are so illuminating that it is worth recording a few. They include:

1585: Six pence "for drinke to the ringers".
1587: 3s 4d for making the lyche gates.
1593: 3s 4d to the Ringers which did ringe for the Queenes holydaye.
1599: 4d spent of the churchwardens one daie fetching the clock from the smithey and settinge it upp.
1601: one shilling paid according to the oulde custom for a ffoxe head. (Foxes were considered a nuisance and had a price on their head. This would seem to be a very generous payment. The authorities apparently recognised this for the price never seemed to go up. Sixty years later they were still paying only 1s).
1606: 8d paid for wyne to serve sicke foulkes in the parish and women with child.

1612: 12d gyven to a poore man of Knotsford that had a certyfycat from the Townesmen that his smithy was brenned (burned).
1612: 8d gyven to a poore man who went to the King with a petycon. (One wonders how such a poore man was able to get to see the King).
1623: 2s payde for wyne which Sir John Dale (curate) had to visit the sicke folkes with.
1642: 9s paid unto the ringers for ringeing upon the King's holiday. (The rate had improved quite considerably from 1593, unless it was simply that King Charles 1 was more generous than Queen Elizabeth).
1655: 24s received from the Hawthorne (hall) for the poore of Wilmslow.
1661: 1s paid for slating the church after the great wind.
1669: £1 17s paid for a blacke (cloth) to lay uppon the dead corpses for the use of the Parishners.

The register made it possible to trace the increase in the number of inhabitants who paid a levy. If the eponymous Mr Gladstone was among these he may well have questioned whether he was getting value for money. He is known to have described the church services as "depressing" and cheered himself up with "athletic exercises" and long walks.

At one time, before alterations, there was no west door, the main entrance being on the south side. In keeping with the centuries-old tradition, another big cash-appeal for repairs was made a few years ago and raised around £75,000.

The Rectory, too, had its fair share of problems. Some historians believe there may have been an original rectory outside the church at the bottom of Church Street. A much larger rectory stood on the site of the present one. It was like a big manor house with 21 rooms, a courtyard, gate-house and outbuildings.

Derelict, vandalised, unloved and unwanted, the former Rectory stands in a sorry state in the late 1970s. The Rev. Edward Beresford had it built in 1778 to replace a previous tumbledown building. Happily it was restored to its original glory by the Natwest Bank. In August 1988 it was sold to Scholes Plc and in 1995, it was back on the market again.

The many-gabled Hawthorn Hall was built in 1698 although its origins go back to the 13th century. It was a boarding school for many years and is now private offices. The hall is reputed to be haunted with ghosts looking for hidden treasure.

In the late 16th century some rooms were used as a school and there is a record of "13d spent by church-wardens on a scolemaister".

Inevitably the place started to crumble and the Rev. Edward Beresford wrote to the bishop saying it was so bad it was "necessary to pull it quite down". The demolition men moved in and it was replaced in 1778 by the new rectory which stands there today. The Rev. Edward Donovan Reeman, Rector from 945 to 1969, introduced cricket in the grounds after the last war. Eventually the new building also suffered from decay and was badly vandalised when it became empty about 1976. There were long debates about what should be done with it until the Natwest Bank took it over and restored it. Some thought the price of about £18,000 was cheap, but the building needed a lot of spending on it. The premises, used for commercial purposes, have changed ownership once or twice since then.

Over a century ago, when a large proportion of the population were worshippers, churches probably outnumbered pubs – although it would be unrealistic to suggest that they were more popular.

They included: the Friends Meeting House (1831); the Congregational Church (1844, enlarged 1863); the Baptist Chapel, Brook Lane, (1890) the Unitarian Chapel in Dean Row, (1962, restored 1845); St Teresa R.C. Church, Morley, (1875); The Wesleyan Chapel in Water Lane (1884, an earlier chapel having been built in 1798); the Methodist New Connexion Chapel, Hawthorn Street, (1870); Mill Brow Mission built beside the present remembrance gardens around 1900 and demolished in the late 1920s.

When the Congregational Church alterations were made in 1863 – all very modern with central heating and gas lights – families rented pews at between 5s and 2s 6d a quarter, according to situation. Soon the place was a sell-out, and once again the down-trod-den poor got pushed to the uncomfortable seats in the galleries.

Skooling Sloly Katches On

Gladstone was fortunate to have had a good education, for proper schooling did not start until 70 years after he entered Parliament. Schools were run either privately or on religious lines. It was not until 1880 that education for the under-12's became compulsory, but for many years after that it continued to be the rich who had far better standards than the poor.

The first village school in Wilmslow was built in 1741 on Station Road. Ninety years later the "children of the poorer classes" found a benefactor in the new rector, the Rev. William Brownlow, who built the Old National School on Parsonage Green for 120 pupils. It taught grammar, algebra and Latin and even in those days they were conscious of keeping costs down. Older boys used to teach young ones.

Boys were taught in a lower room and girls upstairs. "Moonlighting" was not uncommon in those days either – some of the teachers had other jobs like shoemaker, ironmonger and parish clerk. Perhaps one reason why they preferred not to spend too much time in the school was that it was a very damp place with water running down the walls, and the sanitation was said to be unspeakable.

By the 1860s there were a number of boarding schools. Lindow Common Controlled School opened in 1863 – the "common" is said to have referred not to the area but to the fact that the children were from "common people". Children paid three pence a week and a teacher got £25 a year. Five years after it opened it was reported to be "going well". It had 400 "volumes" and had a night school for sewing and reading.

The grandest of the boarding schools were un-

Pownall Hall, now a private school, was formerly the residence of the Fittons, the Pownalls and the Boddingtons. It dates back to 1200 and was rebuilt in 1830.

Many local residents will have nostalgic memories of Wycliffe Avenue council school, off Water Lane. It opened its doors in 1910 and closed several years ago when it was decided that the site would be more useful for housing.

During the last war there was a Church Army canteen for the Forces beside the church.

doubtedly Hawthorn Hall and Pownall Hall. Hawthorn, once known as Harethorn, dates back to the 13th century but the present building was erected in 1698. It is now a grade 1 listed building used as offices and reputed to be haunted with ghosts looking for hidden treasure. There is also said to be an underground passage leading from the hall to the parish church. It became a boarding school in 1835 and was advertised as Hawthorn Hall Classical, Commercial and Mathematical Academy which prepared pupils for "the learned professions and mercantile pursuits".

It taught, among other things, Latin, Greek, French, German – and astronomy. Victorians, apparently, were quite intrigued by things like stars, comets and galaxies. The Academy claimed that the mode of teaching "avoids the drudgery of the old system and the superficiality of the new" (whatever that meant). It said: "The utmost care is taken that the pupil should thoroughly understand the reasons for everything as he proceeds". With all this, plus "magnificent" cricket and football pitches – and no corporal punishment – what more could a boy want? What his father had to pay is not stated.

Pownall, an opulent building with fine carvings, was known as a grammar school when it was founded in 1895. It started life as a manor house in 1200 and was the home of the Fittons for several centuries. In 1830 it was bought by James Pownall of Liverpool who pulled down the old hall and built the present mansion. The estate was later bought by Henry Boddington.

Fulshaw Memorial School, opened in 1876, is still going strong as Fulshaw Junior School. Among the numerous national schools, built for children from poor families, Chancel Lane School was perhaps one of the most notable. It opened in 1868 as three schools

Two nostalgic schooldays pictures: in this picture, these were the last of the sixth form tutors, led by headmistress Mrs Audrey Smith, at Wilmslow Girls Grammar School in Dean Row before the school became fully comprehensive.

These girls were the last selective sixth form at the grammar school. There were protests when the school, one of the most modern and best equipped in the town, was closed after such a short life. The site was left derelict for several years before it was finally redeveloped as a residential area with shops and flats.

in one, with three head teachers for the 350 pupils – 130 infants, 120 boys and 100 girls. Mr Roy Couchman, the headmaster when it closed in 1960, became head of its replacement, Gorsey Bank County Primary School on Altrincham Road.

He also became the proud possessor of a relic from the old school, part of the foundation stone which he found while exploring in a type of cellar beneath the school. Embedded in it was a sealed bottle containing, among other things, a copy of the Manchester Courier. When Gorsey Bank School was built, the children were invited to suggest items to be buried in a time capsule. They showed commendable initiative in obtaining the signature of Yuri Gagarin, the first man in space. This was duly deposited along with their comics, exercise books and coins.

Just inside the gates of the school, which was built on the site of the old workhouse, are two boulders of about knee height. These were used as "mounting stones" by the horse-riding gentry. An attempt to remove them when the workhouse closed was fiercely resisted by the warden's wife. The boulders are believed to have been deposited in the area from the Lake District when Ice Age glaciers re-sculptured the earth's crust a million years ago.

Another school which was axed after a comparatively brief but prestigious existence was the girls' grammar school in Dean Row Road, now replaced by a massive residential development. Staff and pupils were transferred to what was the boys' grammar school, now part of Wilmslow High School. The High School then had two sites – Harefield and Thorngrove – which faced the prospect of being bisected by the new by-pass. However, the school has now moved to a single and much-expanded Harefield site after a major rebuilding programme.

The St Joseph's building at Mount Carmel school in Alderley Edge houses the kindergarten and senior library. To the right of the picture is the original building which was used in the first world war as a military hospital. The school has just celebrated its 50th anniversary.

Chapter 7: Hot News

The First Weekly Paper Arrives and the Town gets its own Council

After the poverty and misery of the early 1800s, things started looking up towards the end of the century. Although the links with the textile industry had been virtually severed, the district was rapidly becoming fashionable, mainly due to the arrival of the railway. The gentry were a familiar sight, bowling along in their smart broughams and acknowledging those who respectfully touched their forelocks. Wilmslow Park, once the domain of medieval lords of Bollin, became a setting for fine Victorian manor houses.

Two significant developments were the arrival of a local newspaper and a new governing body. The first edition of the Alderley and Wilmslow Advertiser (note: the 'Alderley' came first) was published on 17th August, 1874. It cost one penny and had four pages, the front page consisting solely of advertisements.

It arrived just in time to report a major controversy about whether Wilmslow should be autonomous. Inhabitants were angry that they were not allowed to manage their own affairs. They hadn't a market and had to go to Stockport. They couldn't complain locally about foul sewage and drainage conditions – it meant a trip to Knutsford. The toll bar was run by an authority in Macclesfield, and if a citizen was unfortunate enough to end up in court it meant a trip to either Altrincham or Macclesfield. No wonder everyone was aggrieved – especially when transport in those days was not exactly of Pullman standard.

A deputation descended upon London to protest to the Local Government Board, which agreed to hold an inquiry at the Swan Hotel. It was packed. The Inspector, Col. Ponsonby Cox, listened to powerful arguments but was apparently not totally convinced. The townsfolk duly learned that their application had failed – but there was a glimmer of hope.

They were told that the claim would be reconsidered if the locals could show that they could handle the town's affairs efficiently. This proved to be not too difficult and the Wilmslow Local Board was at long last set up in 1878 when Disraeli was PM. The bad news was that this board had an austere tradition against extravagance. It thought that social advancement meant increased public expenditure and that was not to be encouraged. (Doesn't that economic philosophy sound faintly familiar?). The good news was that the board lasted only 16 years. It became the urban council in 1894 as a result of local government reorganisation. As previously mentioned, a number of new schools appeared around 1880, following the introduction of compulsory primary education, but it wasn't only scholastic and commercial interests that were developing. Sport and leisure, too, were becoming popular.

Anyone who has taken delivery of a new car will appreciate the look of sheer joy on the face of this local gentleman. He is Doctor John Gilmore, who was apparently so proud that he even asked his chauffeur, Arthur Williamson, to move over for the picture. Taking up the rear are Mrs Gilmore and their son. For those who are technically minded, the splendid motor is the fabled model T Ford, built at Trafford Park, Manchester, from 1911 to 1927. It was Ford's first manufacturing operation outside America. By 1923 the U.S. company was churning out an incredible total of two million models a year. The car cleared the road by almost 11 inches which enabled it to triumph over England's primitive highways. It nipped along at a top speed of 42 m.p.h., zipped through the gears from 0-40 m.p.h. in 25.8 seconds and cost about $145. Ford justifiably claimed it was "the car that put the world on wheels" and transformed motoring from a rich man's pastime to a part of every day life.

Wilmslow Urban District Council.

RAIDS BY HOSTILE AIRCRAFT

PRECAUTIONS TO BE TAKEN.

By the Order of the Secretary of State of the 8th February, 1916, **HOUSEHOLDERS, SHOPKEEPERS,** and others must **EXTINGUISH ALL EXTERNAL LAMPS, FLARES, AND FIXED LIGHTS OF ALL DESCRIPTIONS,** and all Internal Lights must be **SHADED OR OBSCURED,** so that no more than a dull, subdued light is visible from the outside, and no part of the pavement or roadway, or any building, is distinctly illuminated thereby. Householders should put up **DARK BLINDS** to windows, doorways, and skylights. Fuller particulars will be found in the Order which has been published by means of large posters.

If an attack is imminent, the Police will cause the Buzzer at the Gas Works to give a series of short blasts extending over a period of Four to Five Minutes, and at the same time, and for the same period, the Electric Light and the Gas will be alternately lowered and raised in rapid succession, and then both will be ENTIRELY CUT OFF until the danger is passed.

Gas should be immediately turned off at the meter and the Electric Light at the main switch, and persons are particularly warned to see that all Gas Taps are turned off to avoid escapes when the Gas is turned on again. All Electric Switches should be turned off. Candles can be used if absolutely necessary.

Close all doors and windows, and shutters (if any). Extinguish fires in houses and remove oil lamps, oils, and explosives out of the house if possible. Keep a supply of water in pitchers, buckets, wash tubs, baths, &c., for use in case of fire. Refuge should be promptly taken in the cellar, basement, or lower floor.

Persons must not congregate together or remain in the streets. Congregations of persons should disperse quietly, without panic, to their homes or the nearest place of shelter.

The Fire Brigade and Ambulance Men will hold themselves in readiness at the Fire Station. Qualified Nurses willing to render assistance are requested to send their names and addresses at once to Mr. PRIOR, the Deputy Clerk to the Council.

ALL POLICE ORDERS MUST BE IMPLICITLY OBEYED.

PROTECTION AGAINST POISONOUS GASES.—Mix 1 lb. of washing soda in a gallon of water. Dip a towel in the solution, squeeze it out, and apply to the mouth and nostrils.

SAMUEL BOOTH, Chairman of the Council.
February 14th, 1916.   WILLIAM COBBETT, Clerk.

Keep this Handbill by you for reference.

Wilmslow was to get a four-minute warning from the gasworks buzzer if enemy aircraft appeared during World War I. This council notice in February, 1916, warned householders to fill bathtubs with water, switch off gas taps, extinguish all fires, remove explosives out of the house – and then dash into the cellar. They needed to be a bit nippy!

Wilmslow Rugby Club was formed in 1884. Its first playing ground was at Fletcher's Field (Fletsand Road), followed by Alderley Road near the New Inn and Water Lane. In the early days the team travelled to Sale, Altrincham or Cheadle by wagonette. A diarist of the day recalls that "we often lost one or two, who had to walk". Even in those days, it seems, rugby players managed to get themselves a bit of a reputation. The club went out of existence in 1901, was re-formed in 1923 at Land Lane and opened its present ground and clubhouse in 1934.

Two years after the rugby club was launched, the Wilmslow Choral Society was formed and held concerts in the British Workman Hall. As these quickly became very popular the hall proved to be too small and the society moved to the Drill Hall in Church Street. In October, 1889, a small number of gentlemen got together and decided that Wilmslow needed a golf club. They opened one on farmland near the present Alderley golf club and moved to the present course which was then Pownall Brow Farm, in 1903. No doubt members heard tales of fearsome fairways and wretched rough when they sat down at their centenary dinner.

When the Postman always Knocked Thrice

The postman wasn't kept too busy in the mid-century. Only about 100 letters a day were delivered in 1850 bringing in postage revenue of 10 or 12 shillings (one shilling was 5p). Thirty-five years later he was delivering to 2,000 letter boxes. By the turn of the century business was so good that there were three deliveries a day, at 7am, 1.40pm and 5.20pm. Wall letter boxes were cleared sometimes five times a day.

The local gas company tried to persuade residents in 1930 with the rather amateurish slogan "From coal to gas, then your troubles pass". Judging by the number of appliances on the back of this lorry, it seems to have been successful. The first gasworks was built in 1846.

at 9.55, 12.40, 3.50, 7.0 and 8.50. These were the sort of much-vaunted Victorian values which many people would like to see restored today.

The Post Office was in Grove Street which was now steadily expanding. The police station moved to Green Lane and merited the staffing of one inspector, Daniel Robinson, one sergeant and four constables. Prices at this time were not cheap but it was possible for many to afford the occasional little luxury, like a piece of sirloin at 10d a pound. Milk was 3d a quart, coal 12s 6d a ton, tea 2s a pound. A housemaid earned 7s a week and a railway porter 17s 6d.

Traffic problems had begun to loom as early as 1908. A meeting in the British Workman Hall heard that there was congestion in Dean Row and dust nuisance from "motor lurries", although one would imagine that horses and carts would be just as troublesome. The owner of a steam car was fined 10 shillings for emitting too much smoke. Apparently he had been unable to obtain decent quality coke and had unwisely decided to use coal. The consolation what that it cost him only one penny to post his fine.

Progress was only temporarily interrupted by the First World War. The apprehensive council feared

The Palace Cinema, next to the Railway Hotel, used to be very popular. The main features showing when this picture was taken was 'Destination Gobi' starring Richard Widmark and Don Taylor. These were the days when almost everyone went to the pictures at least once a week. Today film fans go to the video shop instead. (See also page 9.)

Alas, the Palace in Station Road is now long gone, one of hundreds of cinemas throughout the country which eventually found it could not compete with the telly. Sadly, the Railway Hotel has also gone, demolished to make room for yet more offices.

Barons Court, in Bank Square, another fine example of the attractive office blocks which have sprung up in the town in recent years. It replaced the derelict shops shown in the photograph on page 32.

that the Kaiser, rather than the demolition men, would be responsible for buildings disappearing. In February 1916 they issued a handbill to all households warning of precautions to be taken in the event of "raids by hostile aircraft".

It said police would cause the buzzer at the gasworks to give a series of short blasts for four or five minutes. Electric light and gas would be alternately lowered and raised and then cut off. Recognising that unwary inhabitants were more likely to be blown to pieces by their own gas ring than by enemy bombs, the leaflet wisely added: "Persons are particularly warned to see that all gas taps are turned off to avoid escapes when the gas is turned on again".

There was also a do-it-yourself hint on what to do in case the enemy dropped poisonous gas: "Mix 1lb of washing soda in a gallon of water. Dip a towel in the solution, squeeze it out, and apply to the mouth and nostrils". It is hard to resist having a chuckle at the thought of grandad coughing and spluttering his way up the cellar steps and trying to find out where gran had put the washing soda.

During the following years the town and the population grew steadily. Although well-known landmarks like the Vine and the Ring o' Bells in Church Street disappeared, new buildings started springing up. One of the most popular was the Palace Cinema next to the Station Hotel. It was small and typical of the time with, at the back of the stalls, a tiny gallery containing just a few rows.

Most people went to 'the pictures' regularly. They were also being shown in the public hall next to the Swan Hotel. Cinemagoers actually had a choice in those days – you could see different films at different cinemas, instead of the circuit arrangement we have today. It is not clear how long the Palace remained

This was the programme for the Rex's gala opening night on 15th October, 1936. There was the Gaumont British News, a band, a play by the Green Room Society, and heart-throb Errol Flynn in Captain Blood. A matinee seat in the stalls for ordinary shows cost 6d.

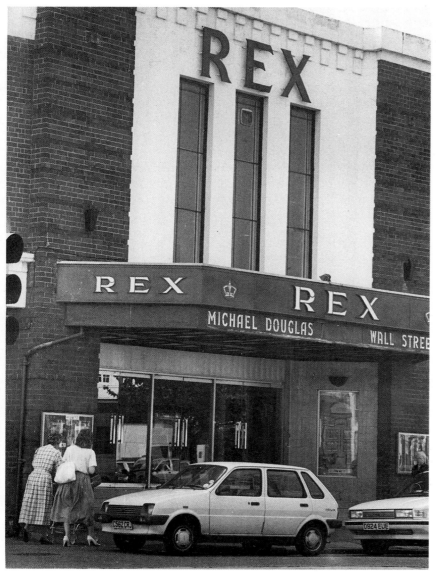

he Rex Cinema, Wilmslow's best-known landmark, died peacefully and unexpectedly after long illness. Will be mourned by thousands of townsfolk.

open, but a much bigger theatre, the Rex, was built some years later on a greenfield site. Hoopers (formerly Finnigans) then was just an allotment.

The Rex had a grand opening on 15th October, 1936, by Mrs Walter Bromley-Davenport and the audience had a splendid evening. There was the good old Gaumont British News, music by a brass band, a one-act comedy called *"Caramels"* by the Green Room Society, and a typical adventure film, *"Captain Blood"*, starring Errol Flynn and Olivia De Havilland. The proceeds were given to the Duchess of York Babies Hospital at Burnage.

Normal prices ranged from nine pence in the front stalls to two shillings in the front circle. (I seem to remember the rear stalls being most popular in my youth). The Rex was a dual purpose building to enable stage productions to be given by local theatrical groups. In post-war years the cinema boomed. It was the habit to go there at least once a week, until, of course, television came along to seduce people in their lounges with quiz shows and 'soaps'.

However, with the demise of the Palace Theatre and Opera House in Manchester, professional plays became popular at the Rex, with stars like Brian Rix, Eric Sykes and Jimmy Edwards, Wilmslow folk, being conservative (with both a capital and small 'C'), flocked to see farces and Agatha Christie thrillers, but turned up their noses at Shakespeare and Ibsen.

Reports of the death of the two Manchester theatres were, as they say, premature, and to most people's surprise, they enjoyed a revival as dramatic as anything seen on stage. Sadly, it meant the end of productions at the Rex. As cinema audiences declined, the Rex underwent a major reconstruction, providing just a small cinema upstairs, seating 328 instead of the original 876. Townsfolk were shocked and saddened to learn during 1995 that the cinema's future was in serious doubt. Director Mr John Stansby announced that the cinema was closing on June 6th 1995, as it was no longer viable. It was the end of "An Awfully Big Adventure", the last film, starring Hugh Grant. He was hopeful that a redesigned cinema would reopen under new management as part of a new shopping development but, at the end of September, it was announced that plans were being prepared to convert the old cinema into a conference centre. This would include a lecture hall with film facilities and seating for around 150. In its heyday, the Rex attracted weekly audiences of around 5,000. As an era came to an end, the total had tumbled to around 600.

No reprieve for town cinema
REX LIFTS CURTAIN ON TALK SHOP BID

Headline from the *Wilmslow Express Advertiser* of September 28th, 1995

Chapter 8: Wilmslow Goes to War

It's Defeat on Overspill, Victory Against Takeover

World War 2 left its mark on Wilmslow in the shape of a disused RAF camp, several austere servicemen's homes, and not a few happy memories among the local maidens of liaisons with Ringway parachutists who dropped in from time to time. It also left a big housing problem which was responsible for the first of two major controversies which hit Wilmslow after the war. Manchester council was short of building land for housing. Wilmslow had plenty of surplus land and it seemed a simple solution for Manchester to build there.

However, Wilmslow was a commuter town for the executive class and residents in their neat suburban homes were not at all happy about having a big council estate in their midst. They were accused of being snobs. The controversy brought passionate debates: To what extent should the town be responsible for the displaced population of the neighbouring city? Shouldn't it have a social conscience? Surely it was dangerous to set up social barriers? Eventually the opposition had to cave in and the massive Colshaw Farm estate was built. Would it be to fatuous to speculate that with today's inner-city decay and expansion of the suburbs, soon Manchester might be asked to accommodate some of Wilmslow's overspill?

Colshaw residents complained for years afterwards that they had just been dumped in a wilderness without sufficient amenities or facilities. Indeed, it is only now, with the development of huge, new private residential estates nearby, that the obligatory supermarket, pub and shops have arrived. Nevertheless they had much-needed homes, and, to everyone's great relief, they were not marooned in high-rise flats. The effect on the town was quite dramatic. In a decade, (1961 – 1971) the population increased by 30 per cent from 22,000 to 29,000.

In 1972, the town faced an even worse threat. The unthinkable happened. Horror of horrors, the Government wanted Wilmslow gobbled up by the Greater Manchester council. However divided the members of Wilmslow Urban Council may have been on other matters, this was certainly one which united them. The takeover had to be stopped at all costs. Leaflets were distributed to thousands of households explaining how disastrous it would all be: Wilmslow was outside the metropolitan concept. It had no affinity with Stockport, to which it would be attached. The effect on rates would be catastrophic. House values could be hit, etc.

Who could fail to be persuaded by arguments like this? Well, the local MP, actually. Mr John Davies was Secretary of State for Industry, and although he expressed sympathy for the cause, he was a dutiful member of the Cabinet. Wilmslow was not beaten.

TO WILMSLOW HOUSEHOLDERS FROM YOUR COUNCIL

WHY YOU SHOULD SIGN
THE PETITION TO REMAIN IN CHESHIRE.

1.   The Government have stated officially that they wish the new local authorities to be related to areas "within which people have a common interest through living in a recognised community". Your Council claim that Wilmslow is a recognisable community in its own right.

2.   An earlier referendum clearly indicated that the residents of Wilmslow desired to remain in Cheshire and this view was supported by the County Council. If democracy means anything at all these wishes should be respected. Signing this petition will re-inforce our views on the most important decision ever to be made on the future of our town.

3.   There are no organisational advantages in becoming part of Greater Manchester. On the contrary Wilmslow is already the administrative centre of many north east Cheshire services such as the headquarters of the regional library, town planning and the social services. We are thus able to deal with our own local affairs on a personal basis.

4.   Both socially, historically and geographically we are linked with Cheshire. In the proposed regional water authorities for example Wilmslow is to be included in the Bollin watershed and grouped with Macclesfield.

5.   Greater Manchester will have a population of nearly 3 million and the Stockport group to which it is proposed we shall be attached has a population of 330,000 including 30,000 from Wilmslow. This new Stockport group will elect sixty-nine councillors of which Wilmslow will have a mere six representatives and in the Greater Manchester Council we are only entitled to one member. By remaining in Cheshire we shall probably have a much stronger representation which could possibly be three times as great.

6.   This increased representation will help to preserve the Green Belt, have more influence on housing development and help to maintain the character and pleasant environment of Wilmslow.

7.   Without exception all the arguments used by the Government in favour of Wilmslow going into Greater Manchester apply with equal force to Alderley Edge which is rightly staying in Cheshire. Why this discrimination?

8.   It is believed that by going into Greater Manchester the effect on our rates could be catastrophic.

9.   Local Estate Agents maintain house values could fall if we are included in the Greater Manchester conurbation.

IN VIEW OF THE ABOVE WE ASK FOR YOUR SUPPORT

BY SIGNING THE PETITION.

The urban council distributed this leaflet in 1972 urging residents to back the campaign to fight being taken over by Greater Manchester. Ninety-three per cent of householders contacted voted to stay in Cheshire and a petition signed by 10,000 people helped to win the fight.

Despite being labelled once again as snobs, the councillors stepped up their campaign. They argued that two thirds of Wilmslow was in the green belt; the town had only 3.8 persons per acre; Alderley Edge had only 6.4 persons per acre. It wouldn't stay like that under Manchester.

The good citizens of Wilmslow were not difficult to convince. No fewer than 93 per cent of the householders who were contacted, voted to stay in Cheshire. In September a powerful document opposing the takeover was sent to the Department of Environment. On 9th October a petition signed by 10,000 people was handed to the Prime Minister. This did the trick. A month later the triumphant councillors heard that they had won ... but there was a price to pay. The Local Government Boundary Commission decided that Wilmslow could stay in Cheshire – as part of Macclesfield. Many would assert that Wilmslow has no more affinity with Macclesfield than it has with Stockport. But at least they are grateful to have escaped the clutches of Manchester.

This handsome office building, Norcliffe House, on the station approach is one of several new commercial premises which have added to the attractiveness of Wilmslow.

Ladyfield House, to the left of the station approach, is another attractive brick-built design blending in well with Wilmslow's town-centre buildings. A competition to name the building was organised by Sema Group, present tenants of both buildings, and the prize, a personal computer, went to Wilmslow High School.

An aerial view of the extensive Zeneca complex at Alderley Park.

The handsome Fulshaw Hall, built by Samuel Finney in 1684 has been renovated by the Refuge insurance company.

No Block On Offices

Recent years have seen a considerable growth in the development of commercial offices. New blocks seem to spring up almost overnight on main roads and in quiet corners. There should be few complaints (apart from inevitable traffic frustrations) if they are all as attractive as those on the station approach and the splendid Refuge Assurance offices at Fulshaw Park.

The designers of the Refuge building took great care to mould their premises as inconspicuously as possible into the parkland. The 700 workers cannot have too many regrets about leaving the grand marble palace in Manchester, which did not lend itself to the new world of high technology (nor, I suspect, to the high rates). Planners promised that the offices, built with 600,000 hand-made bricks and Welsh slates, would not intrude. The car park is partly underground and hidden by trees; there are man-made undulations surrounding a newly-created lake with a fountain. The hall itself underwent a face-lift and was used for some time as a training centre. Its founder, Samuel Finney, would have approved. Wilmslow folk will be gratified that the civic-minded company also contributes to the community, supporting rugby and opera groups, helping church fund-raising, and even sponsoring a local girl to go to the paraplegic Olympics in Korea.

The Refuge is by no means the only company to help the community. ICI, now re-named Zeneca, moved into Alderley Park in the late 1950s and now employs a total of 2,400. They, too, landscaped the grounds and tastefully incorporated new buildings with the old. It even has its own pub, the Stanley Arms. Over the years it has helped many groups, such as scouts and the Northern Chamber Orchestra. It also gave £60,000 towards the East Cheshire Hospice at Macclesfield which is used by local people.

One company which put Wilmslow on the global map was Umbro, which was founded way back in 1924. Their familiar logo on soccer players' shirts and tracksuits is seen by television viewers all over the world. Unfortunately, the company closed their premises on Water Lane and moved to Wythenshawe.

Looking as if it should be on the banks of the Thames at Henley, this is the staff restaurant, complete with trout lake, at the Refuge Assurance Company's offices in Fulshaw Park, Wilmslow.

Chapter 9: Alderley has the Edge

Influential Citizens, Up-Market Homes – and Just a Little Aloof

While Wilmslow rushes to plunge excitedly into the advancing tide of modernity, Alderley Edge sits back, waiting dispassionately for the waves to lap its ankles. It knows it cannot turn the tide back, but it is not going to welcome it unreservedly.

After all, Alderley has a proud and impressive pedigree. It was mentioned (as Aldredelie) in the Domesday survey. And it basically started life as an up-market village "with substantial, picturesque villas, principally owned and inhabited by influential citizens of Manchester and other gentlemen, induced by the pure air, fine scenery and railway conveniences to settle here".

Many fine examples of mansions, with their ostentatious turrets, towers and long drives, still exist, but most have become hopelessly uneconomical and are divided into flats or converted into schools and hotels. The good folk of Alderley, with its quaint antique shops, gastronomic eating houses, trendy wine bar and elegant dress shops, would concede that it is slightly aloof, but deny that it is snobby.

They are determined to avoid having its refined, gentle style and dignity tainted by an modern, vulgar developments. The philosophy, which some would respectfully suggest was just a teeny bit selfish, was spelled out by Cheshire County Council in its document, The Edge Policy, in 1973. It declared:

"Recent infill development cannot continue indefinitely without permanently altering the basic character of the area. Narrow, winding roads are an integral part of the Edge's character. Improvements should be kept to a minimum standard, suitable for present day needs". Which seems to be another way of saying: If we have got to have progress, let's progress as little and as slowly as possible.

What sort of stock do the natives of Alderley come from? The views of William Norbury, a noted writer in his day, are illuminating. In 1884, having observed them for 50 years, he described the citizens in fascinating detail.

They had, he noted, physical peculiarities – long head, projecting eyebrows, high cheek-bones, strong, coarse limbs, Gypsy's skin, slow motions and leaden aspect. They were good poachers, clever at making snares, bee-hives and straw-work. Generally they were harmless, but when exasperated would fight with anything to hand – "some would fight with their mouths or bite like bulldogs". Norbury adds that they shunned society and were almost destitute of religion; they were very sly and suspicious, a race distinct from the rest of the country.

Bearing all this in mind, it would therefore be prudent for any Alderley resident today, next time he meets his neighbour over the garden fence, to take

ll dressed up and no doubt feeling very excited, this Sunday school party from the Hough Chapel prepare to set off on their annual outing to ongleton Park about 1900. The transport was kindly loaned by a local farmer. The chapel celebrated its 150th birthday in 1988.

his pretty road in Nether Alderley, aptly amed Artists Lane, has not changed uch over the years. The chocolate box ene has been painted on many canvases. he attractive cottages on the right are still ere. They are White Gate Cottage and nne's Cottage. Sadly, the lane will lose me of its tranquillity when the by-pass built.

close look at his cheekbones, inquire whether he eats much rabbit, and note how often he goes to church. Above all, decline any entreaties to lend him a fiver – taking great care not to exasperate him.

The oddly-shaped Beacon, with its commanding position 600 feet up on the Edge, was used for signalling purposes and is believed to have been used to send warnings of the Spanish Armada 400 years ago. It collapsed in a gale in 1931.

Notwithstanding the peculiarities of the natives Alderley is a place that attracts thousands of visitors at weekends, summer and winter alike, just as it did 150 years ago. The only difference today is that they generally come by car instead of train. They home in like Exocet missiles, on the Edge, a wonderland of caves and dells, glades and shady paths, thickets spinneys and ice cream vans. With romantic names like Wizard's Well, Stormy Point, Castle Rock, Wind mill Wood and Picnic Rock, it has predictably in spired volumes of fairy tales – notable those of Alderley author Alan Garner.

The historian Ormerod described the Edge as "an abrupt and elevated ridge, which bears the appear ance of having been detached by some great convul sion of nature from the hills". A great sandstone bluff with splendid views across the Cheshire plain, it was once just a desolate heath of gorse and bush. Those taking a pleasant stroll through the 200 acres of woodland should offer a silent thank you to Thomas Stanley, who, in 1660 was the first Cheshire gentle man to be made a baronet.

It was he who planted the beech woods in the early 17th century. Apparently he was concerned at the lack of trees, although the Domesday survey de scribed Aldredelie as a wood three miles long and three miles broad. Presumably the trees were chopped down for fuel. A hundred years later many Scottish firs were added, and today, the National Trust, which owns the land, is carrying on the good work, having planted thousands of saplings in the last few years. A large part of the Edge was open common up to 1779 when it was enclosed. The forest came in useful in 1978 when Granada TV used it for locations to make a play about the signing of the Armistice after World War I.

The entrance to the West Mine, which was started in 1857. It was the biggest and had 2 miles of passages. Some miners are said to have found their way into the cellar of the De Trafford Arms. It yielded 4,000 tons of copper over a period of 20 years and was finally sealed in the late 1950s.

The Wizard Inn, (now restaurant) on Macclesfield road, which was formerly the much smaller Miners Arms. In 1840 Sir James Stanley withdrew its licence when miners were found drunk there. Happily it is now restored and has been used for some years as commercial premises.

Another Fine Mess for the Stanleys

The Stanleys, one of the oldest families in England, held the manor of Over Alderley for 500 years and Nether Alderley for 300 years. They seem to have tried to outdo Cromwell in knocking places about a bit. Originally they lived in Alderley Hall, a huge, palatial residence in Nether Alderley. The date of its origin is unclear but it is known to have been rebuilt in 1570 and again in 1710.

Sadly it was burned down in 1779 and the Stanleys moved to Park House which was duly enlarged. Then, only 39 years later (yes, you've guessed it) they created a mess yet again when they pulled it down and rebuilt it. Nearby woods were later opened to the public on three days a week. The Stanleys link was finally ended when the estate was sold in 1938. Four cottages, now demolished, were let at between £6 12s and £13 a year. Since the late Fifties it has been the home of what was ICI, now Zeneca.

Looking across the plain from Stormy Point towards Manchester and Stockport, the Derbyshire hills are easily visible. Looking towards Chester, it is possible to see the Welsh mountains on a clear day. Near Stormy Point is Castle Rock, which is reputed to be the foundations of an abandoned castle, but like many of the theories about the Edge, it is probably just a bit of romantic fantasy. However, gun flints found there, are genuine relics from the civil war.

Underneath the overhanging rock is the Wizard's Well, whose water is said to have magical powers to cure infertility (well, it makes a change from the usual rheumatism.) It has the face of a wizard carved on it and the inscription:

Drink of this and take your fill,
The water flows by the wizard's will.

Linked to this is the oft-repeated Legend of the Iron Gates. The story goes that a farmer travelling from Mobberley to Macclesfield was stopped on the Edge by a man in a long flowing gown who wanted to buy his white horse. The farmer declined, but on the way home later he was accosted again by the same man who lead him to a rock which he tapped with a wand. A big pair of iron gates arose, revealing the entrance to a deep cave. The old wizard, (named Merlin, naturally), took him inside where there were a number of white horses, several men and heaps of treasure. The wizard paid the farmer for his horse and told him that one day the men and horses would decide the fate of a great battle and save the country.

The tale, still handed down today, was first printed in the Manchester Mail in 1805, but before that it had apparently been first told by Parson Shrigley, rector of Nether Alderley, in 1753. What is not generally known is that similar tales were also being spread around other parts of Britain at the time and may have originated in Europe. Apocryphal or not, it added to the romantic mystique of the Edge.

In contrast, there is nothing equivocal about the history of the beacon. The Edge, being more than 600 feet up, with a commanding position over the countryside, was an ideal spot on which to build the beacon for signalling purposes. It is known to have existed in 1758 and is thought to have been used 400 years ago to flash warnings to other beacons at Helsby and Frodsham of the Spanish Armada.

Originally it was a square room with a door and had an iron pot filled with pitch and tar for signalling – there were no trees to obstruct the view. At the time of the threatened French invasion it was visited by the Duke of Gloucester, the district commander-in-chief. In 1779 Lord Stanley rebuilt it and erected a conical monument on top of the room. Sadly, over the years, it was allowed to deteriorate and the whole place collapsed in a gale on Christmas Eve, 1931. There is now only a small token monument remaining – mums and dads could spend a jolly afternoon letting their kids try to find it.

If they want a few clues, they should pop in first at the National trust visitors centre (check opening days) beside the Wizard car park. Here, you can also ask about places like the druid's ring of stones and the Devil's Grave where Hallowe'en revellers gather each year (and cause a headache for the warden.) There is also a walk for the disabled.

Mines of Information

Here is a brain-teaser, which may appeal to devotees of *Trivial Pursuit*: What is the fourth place in the world, besides Colorado, Ethiopia and Israel, in which a particularly rare combination of minerals and rock is found? The answer is (I have it on the authority of an eminent geologist) – Alderley Edge. The Romans, who were no fools, may have had an inkling of this, for they did their share of digging about under the Edge in AD 43, as did Bronze Age man centuries earlier.

The mines were worked for about 130 years from 1790 and were opened and closed intermittently by a number of different owners. Apart from veins of copper and lead found near the surface, there was also cobalt and traces of iron, silver and gold – very minute quantities, so don't bother dashing up there with your pick and shovel. Miners' jobs in 1792 were described as "a most unwholesome employ, for which the workmen are meanly pay'd as the best earn 14 shillings per week." Presumably things improved, for census returns of 1861 and 1871 show that several miners had arrived from Devon and Cornwall. Others came from North Wales – Anglesey in particular – hence the lane called Welsh Row, just to the south of Alderley Edge.

There were three mines – the Engine Vein Mine, a great gash in the rock, which was the smallest and oldest; the West Mine, which had a quarry-like en-

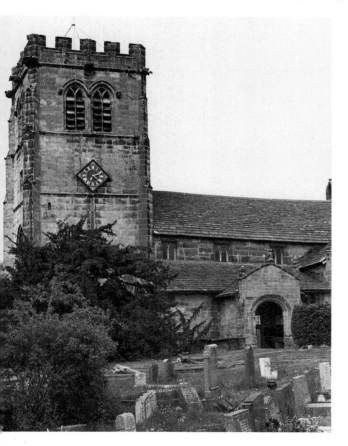

The splendid, 14th century St. Mary's Church at Nether Alderley is one of the prettiest in the county. Various parts were added on over different periods.

The old mill at Nether Alderley, on the A34, dates back to 1391 when the locals used to grind their corn there. Although it fell into disrepair just before the war, it is now owned by the National Trust and has been restored to full working order. There is a regular flow of visitors.

This charming picture of a bit of old England shows the old thatched smithy at Bradford Lane, Nether Alderley, in 1896. It disappeared some 80 years ago and another attractive property, Smithy Cottage, was built behind it, opposite the county primary school.

trance and was the biggest; and the Wood Mine. The West had 12 miles of clean, dry passages, but no-one knows how far the tunnels go as they were never properly mapped and some were blocked. Passages extend under the A34 Congleton road and it is said that some miners once found their way into the cellars of the De Trafford Arms. Another passage emerged by the drive to Swiss Cottage, off Mottram Road.

The main chamber is 300ft long and 70ft high and has a constant temperature of around 50 degrees Fahrenheit all the year round. The mine started in 1857, but was exhausted after only 20 years. It yielded 4,000 tons of copper. Ore was crushed by power from a windmill built in what naturally became known as Windmill Wood. This proved to be inefficient and was replaced by a smelting house and steam engine. The mine was finally sealed in the later 1950s. It left a five-acre spoil heap of 250,000 tons.

The Engine Vein Mine was a deep, open cast mine and was last worked during World War I. Besides copper, cobalt was mined and rich seams were discovered in 1805. It was abandoned when better quality minerals were found in larger quantities in North Wales. It is at the rear of the Wizard restaurant, while the other two mines are across the other side of Macclesfield Road.

Wood Mine is the haunt of cavers, and trips down below for small parties are organised by the Derbyshire Caving Club. Having enjoyed an underground exploration myself, I can recommend it to anyone who has a highly flexible back, strong knees, no worries about claustrophobia, and a strong faith in the navigational skills of the guides.

What impresses most is the dryness of the tenebrous passages and caverns. Unlike most underground workings, there is no sign of dripping, slimy walls. The sandstone rock is so compact that in many cases little roof support was needed. Wood Mine is entered via iron rungs down a narrow, vertical shaft which has a padlocked manhole cover. this was built after all previous mineshafts were sealed around 1920 to prevent unauthorised explorations.

A Deadly Adventure Playground

Despite precautions, many visits ended in tragedy for ill-equipped, amateur explorers. The mines, perhaps inevitably, became a deadly adventure playground. Ignoring warning notices, children managed to find ways into the workings, sometimes dropping 50 or 60 feet on ropes. At least 12 people have died.

In 1930 two youths from Stockport found their way into the "sealed" Engine Vein Mine and got lost in a remote part. Their bodies were found two months later – they had died of starvation. No search was made for them because no-one knew they had gone down. In another tragedy, a schoolboy on an organised expedition in the Wood Mine, slipped off a ledge and drowned in the Blue Lake.

One of the miners' favourite haunts was the Wizard Inn, then known as the Miners Arms and much smaller than the present premises. Records show a building on the site in 1320. In 1840 Sir James Stanley found men drunk there when they should have been digging and withdrew the licence. It then sold only soft drinks and teas which must have been a bit of a shock to the system for miners. A restaurant licence was restored in 1952, and The Wizard has long enjoyed an excellent reputation for fine food. The 28 surrounding acres were given to the National Trust in 1938.

Alderley can boast having a market more than 700

There were more hackney carriages outside Alderley Edge station 90 years ago than normally found today. A steam trains pulls way, outside the Queen's Hotel.

Another quiet scene of the station as a horse and carriage and a man on a horse slowly make their way over the bridge.

years ago when Henry III gave a grant for the holding of a Saturday market and annual fair. A market cross was built about 1253 on Congleton Road, Nether Alderley, which is the Alderley of old. Just 200 yards off the main road is the outstandingly pretty, 14th century St Mary's Church, which is regrettably missed by motorists who need to keep a careful eye on the winding road. It was built from an attractive, locally-quarried sandstone.

Various parts were added in different periods, and now not a great deal of the original building remains. The old schoolhouse built in 1628 stands just inside the church gates. Churchwardens' accounts, now in a dilapidated state, start in 1611. Nearby, on the main road, was the Eagle and Child coaching inn, now a private house, which had a licence until about 1870. The estate of the Stanley family, who lived in the park opposite, also contained two other pubs, the Black Greyhound and the Iron Gates.

Across the road, not many yards away, is the old corn mill, where, centuries ago, the inhabitants used to grind their corn by kind permission of the lord of the manor. It dates back to 1391 but was rebuilt nearly 200 years later. It eventually fell into a state of disrepair and stopped working in 1939. Now under the ownership of the National trust, it is restored to working order and attracts a regular flow of visitors – 500 have been known to turn up on a busy Easter weekend. This is all due to the dedicated work of university lecturer Dr Cyril Boucher, an expert on building technology. He spent three years getting it working again.

Up to the mid-19th century, the village was known as Chorley, or Chorlegh, which means peasants' clearing. Before the railway arrived it was mainly an agricultural area consisting of several cottages, a smithy and the De Trafford Arms. This was said to be "large enough to be convenient and small enough to be snug". Landlady Betty Barber brewed her own ale.

The population in 1836 was 1,325 and the Rev. E. Stanley seems to have made it his business to carry out a one-man survey on social trends. He reveals that nearly half the population were illiterate. Twenty per cent could read and a further 36 per cent could both read and write.

Among the population were three gentlemen landowners, 88 farmers, 273 farmworkers and 39 weavers (strangely, no mention of miners). Between them they owned one four-wheeled wagon, 171 carts with two wheels, 116 ploughs, 176 horses, 661 cows, 67 sheep, 320 pigs and 64 bee-hives. There was a tiny settlement in the Hough and in 1835 they raised the astonishing sum of £500 to build a Methodist chapel.

A Nice Little Earner

From this it is possible to deduce that the blacksmith and the publican were on to a nice little earner. So, too, was the mortician. In the period 1833-35 there were 109 deaths – about eight per cent of the population. The main cause of death – 23 out of the 109 – was consumption, a form of tuberculosis which afflicted those suffering from poverty and poor nutrition.

Alderley, like Wilmslow, began to develop quite steadily in the second half of the 19th century after the arrival of the railway. Lord Stanley got fed up with "excursionists" and wanted to fence them out. However, this could not be done on Sundays, when, it was reported, "people sit all along the paths from the Hough to Stormy Point".

Railmen were anxious to have big houses built in the area and one September day there was "a great

The grand but rather forbidding Victorian face of the Queen's Hotel, adjoining the station platform. It accompanied the arrival of the railway and was said to afford "excellent accommodation".

The former Queen's Hotel as it is today, redeveloped into 18,000 square feet of offices, but with the original facade retained.

A large crowd watches the finish of the mile race at the annual sports day at Alderley Edge cricket ground, about 1910.

Dating back to 1330, the charming, moated Chorley Hall is one of the finest old halls in the county and a grade I listed building. It has undergone several face-lifts including the addition of the Tudor wing by the Davenport family.

Looking up Trafford Road from Heyes Lane. With all the changes that have taken place the scene is not instantly recognisable, except, perhaps, to those who have lived nearby for many years.

This is Trafford Road in more modern times. Many of the buildings in the old photograph have gone.

London Road, Alderley, had an attractive and peaceful air when many of the shops and houses had gardens outside their frontages. This view is looking towards the station. On the left is the Almond Tea Room. Another cafe, the Central Tea and Dining Rooms, is on the right, next to Lavender's newsagents, which has a Daily Dispatch bill outside.

Another view of London Road, showing the De Trafford Hotel on the left.

to-do" on ground owned by the De Traffords. It was said there was a large tent and 143 railroad officials dined there. The villas were subsequently built on Trafford lands and those of minor landowners, but Lord Stanley refused to lease land.

The popularity of the railway grew rapidly (as reported near the beginning of the book) and the LNWR ran 11 up and 18 trains down daily. The Queen's Hotel was built, much smaller then, in 1846 and enlarged by the Victorians who added new wings at the front and rear. It had a forbidding face, and unusually, a long, wide corridor stretched from the entrance right down the centre of the 40-bed hotel. It was to afford "excellent accommodation".

In 1961 you could have had bed and breakfast for about £1.65 with dinner for another 75p. The hotel closed after a fire about 1972 and is reputed to have been sold for nearly £1 million after being withdrawn from auction. It was subsequently redeveloped as 18,000 square feet of offices with the front facade being preserved.

Other buildings which appeared were St Philip's Church (1853), the village school a year later, the Wesleyan Chapel, 1863, and the Mission Hall, 1878. St Hilary's was first founded as Alderley Edge High School in 1880 when it was two Victorian semis called Alma House. It dominated the high street for decades and was renamed in 1913. Extensive alterations were carried out in 1977. The Ryleys, a Georgian and Victorian house, was established in 1877.

Nether Alderley school was provided in 1822 by the Hon. Miss Stanley, became the Alderley Girls School in 1903 and Nether Alderley Council Mixed School in 1907. A rather smart school for girls, the Sunny Bank Ladies College, was built in 1850 between Alderley and Wilmslow. Another school, Mount Carmel, has just celebrated its 50th anniver-

sary. The building was used as a military hospital during the First World War. The village got its own post office in 1854.

Around 1880, when Sir Humphrey De Trafford was lord of the manor, the population consisted of "merchants and professional men and the usual proportion of the trading and labouring classes". There were five hostelries: The Queen's, the Trafford Arms, the Royal Oak in Heyes Lane, its near neighbour the Moss Rose Inn, and the Brookfield Inn in Brook Lane which got its licence on September 20, 1867. The Oak, built about 1850 had "four beds for travellers".

Where The Landlord Rarely Called 'Time'

The Moss Rose, hidden at the end of a narrow little road, is unique in that it had only four landlords in the space of almost 100 years. Nicknamed the Drum and Monkey, it was initially an off-licence, one of a row of cottages built in 1861. The licensee, Mr Leonard, got a full licence and the end three cottages were knocked into one to form a pub. After that there were only three licensees in 88 years: Tom Steel was there for 31 years until he finally called 'Time' in 1920; Jack Brown for 24 years, then Mrs Elsie Crossfield and her husband in 1944.

When Mrs Crossfield died in 1987 the pub was taken over by her son-in-law, Peter Herd. During the early part of the century it mysteriously disappeared occasionally from directory records. Fortunately this was only a clerical aberration, and the hostelry – now so much altered that only the bowling green is recognisable – is as hearty as its ale.

The infamous toll gates were also in evidence, one on Brook Lane which was later moved to Wilmslow, and another on Congleton Road near the

The Moss Rose Inn started life as an off-licence in a little row of cottages. It has the unique record of having had only four landlords in almost 100 years.

Trafford Arms. The charge was 2d for any vehicle, considerably cheaper than the Wilmslow toll.

Along with all this activity came more interest in sport and leisure. Alderley cricket and tennis club, was formed in 1870. Hockey was introduced later. Surprisingly, there was even an Alderley Edge Bicycle Club, formed in 1876. The music festival started in 1910 and the golf club in 1907. One of the more notable feats achieved there, which will not be recorded in the annals of the PGA, was a golf marathon in 1984. Four youngsters started at 4 a.m. and played 150 holes before dark, raising £2,000 for charity.

One of the finest old buildings in the county, Chorley Hall, a grade I listed, well preserved, moated manor house, was built in 1330 by Robert De Chorley. Like many ancient stately homes, it underwent several face-lifts involving different architectural styles which left it with an irregular look. The estate passed to the Honfords and then the Davenports in the 16th century.

There were major alterations in 1550. More were carried out by Sir Thomas Stanley who bought it in 1640 and there was another restoration in 1915. The Stanleys kept it until 1938 and it was let to tenant farmers. When it was put up for auction in the 1970s the sale catalogue described it as "the oldest hall in Cheshire", but this may be open to question. It is reported to have fetched £140,000.

By 1926 Alderley had its first bus service to Manchester (fare eight pence); the assembly rooms were built by public subscription and years later the village had its own police station and fire station in Heyes Lane; the ambulance station was on the main road on the present site of Messrs Wallworks. Some roads have been renamed: London Road was Street Lane; Brook Lane was Preston Lane, named after a family of Prestons who lived there in the mid-1500s; Heyes Lane was Jenny Heyes Lane, presumably after another local inhabitant. There's still a cottage called Jenny Heyes.

London Road was widened after World War I and the gardens which stood in front of shops were removed to make the pavements wider. Shopkeepers used to ask customers, "Is it for the toffs?" and craftily put the odd copper or two on the prices. The shops still offer the same cheerful, old-fashioned personal service. One of the few things to have changed – for the better – is the relationship between "the toffs" in their large houses and their employees from more humble homes.

Today, Alderley carries on its tranquil life, interrupted by only the occasional crisis – like the "Clochmerle affair" in 1970 when villagers carried on a long and heated debate on the siting of new public lavatories. The next crisis, which promises to be even more heated, is likely to be the siting of the new by-pass. Hopefully the problems will be solved and the long-awaited road built. Then Alderley, sheltering snugly under its Edge, can go back to the peaceful days of old. It would love that.

". . . Alderley, sheltering snugly under its Edge, can go back to the peaceful days of old."

Chapter 10: Hall's Well at Handforth

Where the Commuter Regards History as a Thing of the Past

The present-day commuter, crawling through Handforth, is unlikely to notice anything more historic than a week-old chip paper, nothing more colourful than a set of traffic lights. What bit of character and individuality the village once had vanished long ago, buried under Manchester's all-devouring urban sprawl, creeping hungrily and seemingly unstoppable. Yet it was not always like this.

Less than 250 years ago Handforth was trembling to the marching boots of Bonnie Prince Charlie's men heading south. Four hundred years ago Handforth Hall was the centre of a highly successful entrepreneurial business that, today, would have been hailed as a first class example of private enterprise.

The Hall, handsome if not awesome, is, of course, Handforth's history. (More details later). It is unseen by the hurrying commuter, just a few minutes' walk from the A34. It stands incongruously, but still retaining its dignity, on the fringe of a modern housing estate and next to the village Roman Catholic school.

Whether it will retain its dignity now that the massive Handforth Dean supermarket development has opened just a trolley-push from its back garden remains to be seen. Urban conservationists generally have to bow to the march of so-called progress, usually receiving an obligatory minor concession.

Local chroniclers through the centuries seem to have had some difficulty with the name Handforth, as they did with Wilmslow. It has appeared variously as Honford, Handford, Hondford, Handeforthe, Hanneford and Handforthe. It is said to have been originally Hanna's Ford, but as no-one knows who Hanna was, it again comes under the heading of Useless Information.

Handforth, originally Handforth-cum-Bosden, was for many years in the parish of Cheadle with which it has strong historical links. The Handforth parish church is St Chad's and in the seventh century a monk called St Chad arrived in the area to preach Christianity. A place called Chad Hill was named after him and this eventually became Cheadle. But we shall not dwell on the ancient history. Instead of starting at the beginning we shall start at the end and work backwards. (I somehow find Agatha Christie easier to read that way – the story seems less confusing).

Documentors seem to have an obsessive fascination with churches. Glance through one or two guidebooks on your bookshelf and you will see what I mean. However, for those of us who are less architecturally minded and who do not get over-excited by descriptions of ornate Gothic archways, it is the olde worlde pubs which usually attract most interest.

One which would most certainly attract the commuter's eye as he waits at the traffic lights in Handforth is the Tudor-style Freemason's Arms. It is easy to imagine Cromwellian parties being held there – but in fact the building dates back only to Victorian times and was formerly in part a humble chip shop.

Conversely, two others which appear to be ordinary modernised hostelries, most certainly have a romantic history. The Greyhound and the Waggon and Horses both date back to the early 18th century and were regular stopping places for horsedrawn coaches when the first turnpike "main road" to the south became operational in 1768.

Decades later, while Alderley attracted "excursionists" by train, visitors to Handforth used to arrive by coach and four from Manchester to view "our lovely village" as one commentator described it. Travellers approaching the Waggon and Horses had to negotiate a toll bar which opened in 1753 and continued to collect pennies for another 130 years.

The gardens present an elegant setting for handsome Handforth Hall, now lovingly and painstakingly restored to its original glory. It was built by Sir Urian Brereton in 1562.

The olde worlde inscription above the Hall's doorway was written by a craftsman who had apparently not passed his English 'O' levels.

Not a commuter in sight! This was the main road through Handforth nearly 100 years ago, with the former parish church on the right. The farm which is now the shopping precinct is in the distance on the left.

These premises on Manchester Road at the Station Road traffic lights have changed little over 100 years although the shops have changed owners several times. The one on the corner had a little garden at the front. On the right was the Manchester and Liverpool District Bank and next to it, S. Green, draper. On the left, the present showrooms opposite the Freemasons, used to be a post office and grocers.

The first Waggon premises were built in front of the present building which was erected in 1938. The pub is unique in having its "cellar" in the roof, the barrels being winched upstairs by a jib. The Unicorn and the Bull's Head are mentioned in records of 1828. The original Bull inn can easily be seen next to the extension.

The Greenery Starts to Fade Away

Incidentally, for those who like to know about such things, the Greyhound is believed to have got its name from the prominent Tatton family whose coat of arms bore a greyhound as its crest. Similarly a family called the Wrights who owned Handforth Hall early in the 18th century had a bull's head as the crest. Perhaps we can leave the origin of the Waggon and Horses to the imagination.

Veterans of the village still talk nostalgically of the days before it all changed and bits of greenery started rapidly to disappear. The Paddock shopping precinct, now attractively refurbished, sprung up on what was then Church Farm. There were dramatic changes in the population and skyline when the Spath Lane estate, with its space-saving tower blocks, was built in 1968 as an overspill for Manchester. This meant that some 7,000 people were now living in Handforth and it soon became obvious that more changes were needed. Six years later the village green was dug up to accommodate the library and health centre, which were naturally very welcome.

From 1830 there were two major places of employment, both on the banks of the River Dean. One was the paper manufacturers of Saxon, Royston and Co., which was established about 1828 beside the main road on the current site of a car servicing centre, formerly an ambulance works. This later became a bleach works. The other was the calico print works of Symonds, Cunliffe and Co. This company occupied the site later used as offices by the Co-operative Society and is now once again scheduled for redevelopment.

Many workers wore clogs as they headed off for a 6am start. A Foden steam wagon and trailer, laden with cloth, chugged its way to Manchester each day at 9am. During the last war the print works served as a tank depot and remnants of tank ramps, mainly hidden by undergrowth, still remain near the Hall. In fields nearby, RAF men from a Maintenance Unit were housed in huts which were only finally cleared away in 1981. This was a massive job – 100 acres being reclaimed, including 20 acres of concrete.

Planners have talked not very enthusiastically of transforming this area into a golf course alongside the new Handforth by-pass, but local dog-walkers in their green wellies suggest that paddy fields would be more suitable. A second camp of wartime airmen sprung up just outside Handforth on Dean Row. This is now a housing estate, and some other austere RAF dwellings have been converted by enthusiastic owners into attractive modern homes.

Maybe they would have liked their children to go to Dean Row County High School (formerly the girls' grammar school) but this, sadly, has now been closed after a lifespan of a mere 23 years. It had served a purpose of educating children from the post-war baby boom. Another landmark with a somewhat longer lifespan of 139 years has also disappeared. The Old Comrades Hall, the hub of social activity for decades, was bulldozed in 1975. It was built by Non-conformist Methodists in 1846 as the Kilham Chapel on the site of the present British Legion car park in Station Road.

In 1920 it was bought as a meeting place for comrades of the Great War, and then during the last war was utilised as a barracks for locally-based troops. The British Legion took it over in 1965 but its

An ancient landmark bites the dust. The Old Comrades Hall, which had started life as a chapel in 1846, was bulldozed in 1975 to be replaced by the British Legion building a few yards further back from the road.

The print works, on the site which later became the Co-op offices, was used as a prisoner of war camp during the first world war. It housed 2,000 prisoners, mostly Germans – twice the Handforth population. To make sure they felt at home, a heating plant was installed.

condition was deteriorating badly and it was closed in 1972 when the new building was completed. However, its memory still lingers on through the Handforth Gala – the first one was organised in the hall in 1968. The Parsonage, not far away, also vanished under a new housing development.

Achtung! 2,000 Germans Arrive in Prison Camp

In World War I the print works figured prominently again. In fact it could justifiably claim to have a history almost as important as the Hall, in its own, much shorter lifetime. At the outbreak of the war the works had some huge, unused sheds, nearly a quarter of a mile long. They were built by the Bradford Dyers Association in 1910, but they abandoned a scheme to establish a plant there. When the war started it was initially intended to use the sheds as a barracks for British troops, but this plan was also abandoned.

Instead, they were converted into a prisoner of war camp for Germans. The first 500 arrived on 6th November, 1914, a fortnight later there were 1,000, and by the end of the month the total was boosted by a further 573 East Africa prisoners. In March, 1915, the Manchester Guardian (as it then was) described in colourful detail the arrival of 600 prisoners captured in the trenches at Neuve Chapelle in France.

Some of the 2,000 German prisoners under guard in Handforth during the first world war. A newspaper report described them as of "excellent physique, sturdy fitness and well-clad appearance".

The health centre and library now stand on this site which used to be the village green.

They received "an unostentatious reception and suffered no humiliation". Only a few inhabitants watched them march past at a swift pace from the station. Bystanders were impressed by their "excellent physique, sturdy fitness and well clad appearance". Certainly they didn't look as though they had just survived an ordeal in the trenches.

They were mainly aged 20-35 and marched with a light, strong step. While the column was forming outside the station, the men gossiped "with great cheerfulness", and waved to a photographer they spotted at a cottage window. Their uniforms were in excellent condition and showed little sign of wear, apart from mud.

Their arrival brought the number of inmates to about 2,000 – double the local population. The post office was overburdened and there was plenty of work for the censor and interpreter. Some men were allowed to work on farms. Local butcher Mr Joe

Hewitt remembers as a small boy collecting bread which fell off delivery carts and "eating stale bread for weeks".

His father, who was a cab proprietor, took wounded soldiers unable to walk, from the station to the camp. There, they found the good old Brits had installed an extensive heating plant. Among the inmates were many civvy aliens who had been living in England when hostilities commenced. It must have felt a comfortable haven from reprisal when the British liner Lusitania was torpedoed with the loss of 1,200 lives on 7th May, 1915.

Railway Puts Village on the Right Lines

In later years the village grew only slowly. Handforth garage was a small wooden hut. It repaired mainly bicycles as there were few cars. On Church Road there was a slaughter house where the village butcher bought his meat. Sagars Road was known as Private Road and locals had to pay to use it. A big house there, called Knowle House, was offered to the local council but it was unable to afford the upkeep. Subsequently it was given to Manchester Corporation as a home for mothers and babies.

A resident of the times tells a delightful story about a wealthy solicitor named Sydney Hope who owned what is now the Pinewood Hotel. He gave away trees to beautify the area and solved the litter problem by giving five pennies to children who picked up paper blowing about.

Following the building of the bleach and print works, Handforth became firmly established in the industrial age. It was helped considerably by the opening of the railway in 1842, five years after Queen Victoria came to the throne. The station was not much more than a shed, with one man selling tickets and stopping trains by signal. But it was the start of a commuter pattern that is a part of every day life today, with home-buyers following the railway track.

The Manchester and Birmingham Railway (later the London and North Western Railway) whisked people into the city in little more time than it takes today's electric coaches. New rows of cottages sprang up, including those near the station in 1885. Finally, at the turn of the century, civilisation became complete when Handforth decided to try to keep up with its more progressive neighbour down the road and replace its oil lamps with gas.

The Wilmslow and Alderley Gas Company agreed to extend its mains to the village which duly became all lit up. Oddly enough, there had been two gasometers in the village for some years but they served only premises nearby. The population by now was growing steadily and approaching 1,000. A parish council had been elected and was soon replaced by an urban council. This in turn was amalgamated with Wilmslow UDC in 1936.

Surprisingly perhaps, in view of the small population in the latter half of the nineteenth century, churches, too, had become well established. Ungenerous observers have been heard to suggest that they had nothing else to do in those days. St Mary's Methodist Church was built in 1872; the present St Chad's went up in the late 1890s to replace the old parish church built in 1837; and of course there was the previously mentioned Kilham Chapel. The church school opposite St Chad's was recently closed after a long battle to save it, and is now converted into offices, still retaining its original frontage. The Dean Row Chapel dates back to the 1600s and is one of the oldest chapels in the county.

A Five-Bed Des. Res. for £20,000

Going back beyond 1700, not a great deal was happening in Handforth. It was just a hamlet with a few assorted peasants, farmers and landowners – and of course, the Hall, which is worth a book all to itself. For decades it was a working farmhouse. Today it owes its existence largely to the enthusiasm and dedication of its subsequent occupants, Mr and Mrs Chris Douglas, and a previous owner, Mr Ian Grange, have painstakingly restored the building.

In the seventies, you could have picked up what appeared to be a bargain: a listed building with four large recep., five beds, hand-carved oak staircase with secret hiding place, extensive grounds and outbuildings – all for around £20,000.

Unfortunately there was the slight problem of having to spend several thousands of pounds more n repairs and restoration. The hall had successive owners who never lived in it and it was derelict from about 1972 to 1976. In 1973 it was bought by a Staffordshire company for £21,000 after it had failed to sell at auction.

They planned a £75,000 face-lift to make it a "nice country pub and eating place". However, there was opposition from planners and local residents and while the debate was going on there was concern about vandalism and the rapid deterioration of the building. Another plan to turn it into offices failed.

Then, in 1975, a company director Mr Grange bought the Hall from Handforth Hall Ltd and over the next three years spent over £40,000 on restoration. The roof was repaired with 40 tons of stone and new leaded light windows costing £3,000 each were put in. Again there was a change of owners and it was not until Mr Douglas moved in with his wife in June, 1982, that the hall's future became assured. He employed many craftsmen to transform it into a beautiful home with attractive gardens that will be around for many more years.

The original hall, believed to date back to the 14th century, was demolished by Sir Urian Brereton who built the present building in 1562. It was much bigger than today with more than 40 rooms. An inventory in 1610 mentioned Mr Leigh's chamber, a knight's chamber and a gentlewoman's chamber. Some say there was a courtyard, but Mr Douglas, who has done his own research, doubts this.

A hand-carved inscription over the main doorway, by someone who had definitely not passed his English O-levels, reads (see p. 86):

(see p. 86)

This haulle was buylded in the yeare of our Lord God MCCCCCLXII by Uryan Breretonn knight whom maryed Margaret daughter and heyre of Wyllam Handforth of Handforthe esquyer and had issue VI sons and II daughters".

Sir Urian was the second husband of Margaret Hondford whose ancestors "ruled" Handforth for 400 years. Margaret was first married, at the age of 12, to Sir John Stanley, the new lord of the manor of Handforth, but this marriage was dissolved in 1530. She and Sir Urian were friends of the manorial family of Bulkeley of Cheadle. They had eight children and the descendants continued to control the manor. Their last daughter, Sybil, married Thomas Legh of Adlington.

It was not until after his wife died that Urian decided to build the new hall to replace the original. Then he married again – this time into another worthy family, the Trafford of Trafford Park. Urian, it seems, was quite keen on expanding the population. His new wife, Alice, produced five more children in addition to the eight from his previous marriage.

After he died in 1577 the hall continued to thrive and through his offspring the manor became highly prosperous over a period spanning about 100 years. The family business drew substantial rents and fees from interests all over Cheshire. They had countless smallholdings, houses, grazing lands, woodlands and corn mills from which it received substantial rental income.

Courts which dealt with poachers, drunks and other wrongdoers, sat in the Hall and dispensed justice. This frequently meant an uncomfortable spell in the stocks. Scolds – women who gossiped too much – were given a ducking.

The most famous of the Breretons was Urian's great-grandson Sir William, an MP and general who was something of a Montgomery in his day. He helped Cromwell win 17th century Civil War battles between king and parliament and seized Chester after an amazing siege lasting more than a year. Sir William died in 1661 and when his only son Thomas went the

Wilmslow Road, Handforth

It seems hard to believe that this was Wilmslow Road, Handforth, at the junction with Station Road. Today, the Freemasons pub is on the right.

same way 12 years later the Hall ceased to be the historic centre of the manor of Handforth. Lands were dispensed with, leaving just a small bit to be farmed by the hall's tenants. Subsequently it had several different owners.

Handforth itself first emerged in 1190 under William de Honford and had strong historical links with Cheadle. A century later, a descendant, Henry,

brought the village its first water mill which inhabitants used to grind their corn for their daily bread. It was built on the River Dean near the former Co-operative Society's premises. If today's commuter parked his car and strolled along the riverside he would come across remnants of old workings. Was it the corn mill? Whatever it was, it shows that Handforth did have a little bit of history.

Chapter 11: Signs of The Times

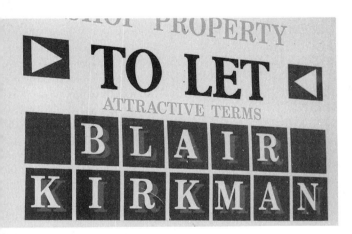

When you reflect upon it, any innovative or different mode of transport invariably seems to have a major impact on people's lives in some form or other. None more so than the arrival of the railway in Wilmslow. Virtually overnight the town was transformed from a sleepy backwater to a vibrant community. Now, just over 150 years later, we have an equally dramatic new arrival – the A34 by-pass. But this time, will it be a blight rather than a blessing? For the huge new out-of-town superstores linked to it, at Handforth and Cheadle, threaten to turn Wilmslow into a ghost town. If you think that's something of a wild exaggeration, take a look at towns like Dudley, in the West Midlands, and Rotherham, South Yorkshire, where the impact has been so severe that the Government has now been forced to do a U-turn and refuse planning permission for similar developments.

Here we have a modern day dilemma. If we don't shift the traffic from the town centre, it risks dying of strangulation. If we do shift it, via a by-pass and huge new shopping centres, it risks dying of suffocation, deprived of shoppers' life-giving oxygen. The answer, of course, is to build the by-pass without the superstores. But then the highways authorities would have to cough up another £25 million or so which the superstores donated, not so much in a rash outburst of altruism, more a case of recognising a nice little earner when they see one.

One obvious solution is to make the town centre more attractive, so that while the commuters and through traffic speed by on the by-pass, shoppers – those who cannot, or choose not to go out of town – can wander round in peace without the fear of being mown down by a homicidal driver. Our worthy councillors debated and argued long and hard about whether to pedestrianise Grove Street. A vociferous minority protested strongly, particularly about the loss of parking spaces (about 50). But, armed with the results of a shopping survey which showed that 75% of those questioned were in favour of pedestrianisation, the scheme got the go-ahead.

It was put out to open tender and the council's own works department can take pride in winning the £420,000 project. Within an 18-week period, 240,000 special, easily-cleaned tiles had been expertly laid followed by the introduction of trees and seats, which became instant targets of mindless graffiti artists rapidly followed by skateboarders and wheelies who saw it as a heaven-sent new playground. (They are now officially banned but there appears to be no-one to police the ban). And so Grove Street took on a smart, relaxed new look. Shoppers could walk peacefully without being bounced off narrow pavements into the path of snarling, fume-belching vehicles. But the doubters quickly questioned whether the transformation would have the desired effect. Was it a case of rearranging the deckchairs on the Titanic? A triumph of hope over bitter experience?

To find the answer it is helpful to study the findings of a fascinating six-month shopping survey, commissioned by the borough council and carried out by the Department of Retailing and Marketing at Manchester Metropolitan University (they call it rather grandly "An Investigation Into The Town's Retail Function"). Objectives of the survey, carried out between October 1993 and March 1994, were to find out WHY Wilmslow had apparently declined as a shopping centre and to suggest WHAT could be done to revitalise it. There was no shortage of volunteers wishing to air their views.

Researchers analysed 1,000 completed questionnaires, interviewed key members of the community, and studied a geo-demographic database. Their findings will come as no surprise to anyone: there are ewer "convenience" retail shops because the town is in the deathly stranglehold of the terrible twins, Sainsbury's and Safeways. It would have been most satisfying to those, like myself, who abhor grocery superstores, if we could have read the following sentence: "We recommend that both Sainsbury's and Safeways be razed to the ground to allow smaller shops to return and survive, and thus promote the resurgence of the town."

Although Wilmslow has a nominal population of about 35,000, the potential catchment area is around 100,000. The profile of the average Mr and Mrs Wilmslow is quite startling, as revealed in the survey's following findings:

- The number of households with two or more cars is double the national average.
- The number of "older couples in leafy suburbs" is more than four times the national average.
- "Young mortgaged families" account for over 30% of households, which is 72% higher than the UK average.
- The owner occupancy rate of 76% compares with 56% nationally.

Probably the most remarkable revelation is what a really affluent lot we Wilmslow folk are: the number of households falling into the (apparently) wealthy AB socio-economic groups exceeds the UK base by nearly 80%. There are almost twice as many professional people and about half as many semi-skilled or unskilled workers. Perhaps surprisingly, the number of prosperous pensioners in town is well below the national average. Apparently four out of five of us visit Wilmslow at least once a week and of these, 61% are female. Two thirds of visitors travel by car. (Very expensive cars, too, it would seem. In one week in 1995 a local garage apparently sold eight Rolls-Royces, six Aston Martins, seven Ferraris and 29 Porsches, all new N-registration cars).

Death of the small trader

With impressive statistics like these to hand, the obvious question to ask is: Why has Wilmslow in general, and Grove Street in particular, lost its "Mayfair of the North" image? The answer lies not in one, but a number of factors. The late eighties were boom years in which major national retailers were fighting to get into Wilmslow and were prepared to pay ridiculous rents, just to maintain market share. The small trader could not compete, particularly as much of his trade was going to the big supermarkets, and had to get out.

At the time of the survey there was no butcher or greengrocer, remarkable for a town the size of Wilmslow. Shop rents were similar to those in Macclesfield but were relatively high when it is recognised that Macclesfield rents are boosted by the presence of "anchor" stores like M & S. Such is the dominance of "Marks" on the high street that no fewer than 70% of those questioned said they missed not having such a store in Wilmslow.

Of course the eighties boom could not be sustained. The bubble burst, the housing market collapsed, the recession followed and so the town started its steady decline.

This is bad news for those of us who are fed up of staring at disused and dilapidated premises which scar the town centre. One suspects that there is an impasse here between the council and developers: the council says "You cannot do that" and so the developer says "Right, I'll let it rot." I am told by the developers of one particularly ugly site that rebuilding will take place "sooner rather than later", whatever that might mean. Obviously they are hoping to find retailers prepared to pay top rents. Unless there is strong pressure by the council to have these eyesores removed, the town is going to face a losing battle to regain its "Quality Street" image.

One of the unenviable tasks of Wilmslow's Town Manager, Diane Smith (who also acts in a similar capacity for Knutsford and Macclesfield) is to use her diplomatic skills to get local businessmen and tradespeople to work together, and with community leaders, to revitalise the town – no mean feat. At long last the seriousness of the situation has been recognised. A working group assisted by council officials has been set up and a PR company hired to come up with ideas to promote the town.

Diane Smith points out that the town has a significant proportion of transient residents, which in turn contributes to a lack of identity for Wilmslow. Both she and the university researchers identify the virtually non-existent nightlife as part of the problem. Both would like to see more restaurants and cafe bars which have given the likes of Knutsford a lively reputation. Traders, too, seem keen on this but for some inexplicable reason there is a body of councillors opposed to the idea. The proportion of service outlets (fast food, coffee shops etc) is 20 per cent lower than the national average. Does Grove Street need four banks, three building societies, two travel agents and an estate agent?

The market comes in for a fair amount of criticism by the university researchers: too small (15 stalls); relatively high rents (£9.00 per week); bad location (cut off by the A34); appearance (shabby state does

These ugly, boarded-up semi-detached houses in King's Close, Wilmslow, are used as a free parking lot by office workers. They have scarred the town centre for years, while planners and developers procrastinate interminably. Doesn't anybody care?

ot encourage people to visit); and no free parking spaces. Yet if it was managed and presented correctly, with something of a continental atmosphere in terms of the mix of stalls, the market could be advantageous.

Just how bad *is* parking in Wilmslow? Well, not as bad as many people think. There are 1,700 parking spaces, including 1,100 in car parks (compared with 2,000 at the new Tesco/M & S site). The trouble is that too many people complain if they have to walk more than 100 yards. The problem, suggests the survey courageously, is all in the mind and therefore people's perceptions must be changed.

There has to be a serious re-think if Wilmslow is to compete seriously with out-of-town stores. Why should someone have to pay 60 pence to do a bit of shopping, and risk a £25 fine if they overstay? In neighbouring areas like Bramhall and Cheadle, short-stay shoppers are encouraged with a 10 pence charge. A lowering of overall parking charges, with a maximum two-hour stay in the most central colour-schemed parks, are measures recommended in the report. Others include eradicating the empty retail eyesores, improving signposting to amenities, revitalising the market, improved pedestrian crossings, and the introduction of "quality" street performers, seasonal festivals and outdoor exhibitions. What are we waiting for? Let Grove Street have, during the warmer months, street cafes, colourful, up-market craft stalls where local artists and artisans can show off their wares.

I suppose it is too much of a Utopian dream to see the banks banished to the side-streets. All we need are a few multi-card cash dispensers, strategically and safely situated, including at the supermarkets and at places which you can easily drive up to. The survey says out-of-town developments, far from being a potential threat to the viability of Wilmslow, should be seen as an opportunity to bring a new vitality to the town. We shall see.

Ambivalence and the By-pass

Such is the power of the conservationist lobby today that it is hardly possible to dig up a blade of grass without a Whitehall mandarin appearing on the scene and setting up a public inquiry. As far as is known, there were no instances of people setting up home in the tops of trees when construction of the A34 by-pass got under way, but that is not to say that there wasn't much opposition. Far from it. (Although one group of protesters in Handforth closed down their fighting fund and withdrew their opposition when the wives suddenly discovered to their delight that the huge new M & S store would be only a few minutes' walk away.)

It wasn't so much that the NIMBY brigade were totally against the by-pass; more an understandable case of 'keep it as far away as possible and shield us from noise and pollution'.

A company of acoustics experts were called in and it didn't take them long to identify Handforth Road, Swinley Chase, Beaufort Chase and Woodlands Road as an area where "the noise climate will increase significantly when the new by-pass opens." There was also the problem of the noise made while construction work was going on. Earthwork operations by dumper trucks and bulldozers, it was estimated, would be relatively low at 47-52 decibels because of noise-shielding effects. The normal limit from construction work is 70 decibels – and that's quite a din. Bearing in mind that locations had to be found for the disposal of 800,000 cubic metres of material it was

Looking down Manchester Road, towards Wilmslow, when weavers' cottages were in abundance.

The same scene today, looking towards the King William, with the new roundabout linking the A34 to the by-pass.

Bollin Walk as it was before the by-pass. One side of the road was demolished to make way for the new link.

Old Road (right) looking down towards the parish church, was used by some stage coaches until the new road, left, was opened up.

essential that noise pollution was kept to a minimum. A mound alongside the carriageway, at least three and a half meters high and planted with thousands of trees, was deemed sufficient to solve the problem.

While the acoustics experts were counting decibels, a team of ecologists were on their hands and knees examining the flora and fauna in minute detail. Their verdict was that the acres south of the M & S site were of "low botanical interest". There were abundant buttercups, some foxgloves, a woodland area of oaks, lime, beech and sycamore, and a few hedgerows "not species-rich, with poor wildlife habitats and of no conservation importance".

Kingfishers were breeding along the banks of the river Dean, but this did not seem to be a problem. What did appear a big problem were the little newts and frogs ... and the badgers. Unless something was done, the newts and frogs and other amphibious creatures would find themselves trying to swim beneath thousands of tons of rubble. Much to the joy, and relief, of the conservationists, new ponds were constructed and the newts and frogs relocated. Anyone visiting the site must have been puzzled by the large rings of plastic sheeting placed around the pond boundaries. These were a clever device to keep them in, just in case they were not too happy with their new homestead and were tempted to try to get back to their old one.

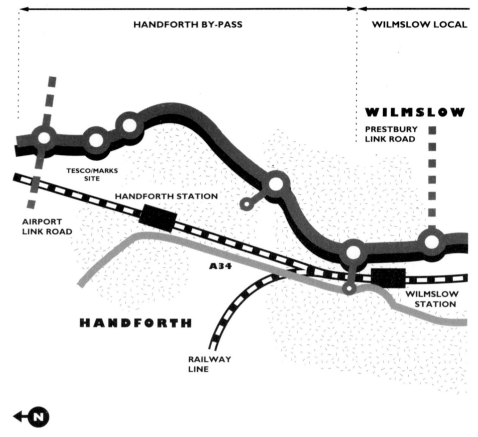

The long-awaited A34 by-pass, which will probably have cost £100 million by the time the Alderley section is completed, in 1998.

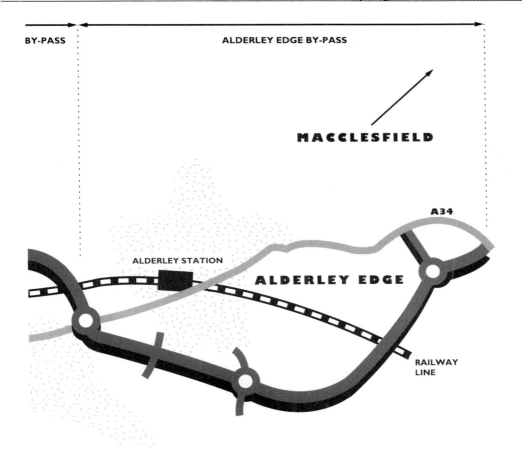

BY-PASS

ALDERLEY EDGE BY-PASS

MACCLESFIELD

A34

ALDERLEY STATION

ALDERLEY EDGE

RAILWAY
LINE

The Alderley nursery of S.E. Matthews grew and planted 85,000 trees and shrubs to keep the conservationists happy. Unexpected problems put the Wilmslow end of the by-pass months behind schedule.

and after the raising of land levels. There was to be no working at night to disturb their nocturnal foraging and the Bollin Valley Project was responsible for the management of the land. Oak and beech trees were to be planted to provide food for the badgers and it was proposed by the survey team that the site should eventually be restored to grazing land with a cocktail of mixed seeds.

For the benefit of anyone with appropriate and sufficient land, and who has always wanted to attract badgers, I will give the recipe: about 50% of perennial ryegrass mixed with roughly equal amounts of common bent grass, crested dogstail, red fescue, meadow fescue, common birdsfoot trefoil, red clover and white clover. That should keep 'em happy! Whether, in fact, the River Dean badgers were still in residence when the by-pass work was completed, alas, I am unable to say.

While this small team was diligently at work constructing new homes for the wildlife, half a mile away a huge army of workmen with bulldozers and trucks

That took care of the newts. What about the badgers? The ecologist team reported the existence of an "extremely active and very large" badger sett. Badgers are, of course, protected by law and these were seen as "of major concern". Apparently they need extensive areas of foraging habitat and it was important that the habitat should be maintained both during

An aerial view showing the Bollin Walk roundabout section of the by-pass nearing completion. A glimpse of Wilmslow station can be seen bottom right; parts of Wilmslow Park and Summerfields are top left. *(Aerial photograph reproduced by courtesy of David Jewell.)*

were transforming a derelict site into a massive new 40-acre shopping area with 2,000 car parking spaces and up to 1,000 very welcome new jobs. Ironically, thousands of commuters travelled daily along the A34 at Handforth, unaware that this huge new complex was taking shape, just a few hundred yards away. The M & S store, with 85,000 square feet of retail space, is one of the biggest single storey stores in the country. Alongside, Tesco has another 52,000 square feet of selling space, together sufficient to attract shoppers from a vast catchment area. In August, as the 12-month project was coming to an end, and roughly on target despite appalling weather at the start of the year, enormous "carpets" of Tarmac appeared as if by magic, embroidered with hundreds of trees.

Within the air-conditioned stores, another small army of workmen installed dozens of rows of shelving which would soon be filled with thousands of items to satisfy the needs of hordes of shoppers, many of

The Handforth Dean site of Tesco, Marks and Spencer, and Allders, has 2,000 car parking spaces, bus stops, and 150,000 square feet of retail shopping space, plus a huge restaurant. It opened apparently on target in October 1995. The development provided nearly 1,000 new jobs - but will it kill off local businesses?

them no doubt deserting the local shops of Wilmslow and Handforth. Further south, work was progressing steadily but less spectacularly, clearly some way behind as far as the carriageways were concerned. However, thanks to good summer weather, rapid progress was made with bridges and access points. One unforeseen problem was the failure of a contractor engaged on bridge work near Wilmslow station and there were fears that this would delay completion of some of the work, incorporating the Prestbury link road, by up to a year.

The Alderley By-pass

For the impatient Alderley Edge residents, their 10-year wait for a by-pass to alleviate frustrating traffic snarl-ups in the village may not end until almost the next century. The two-year project is not due to start until late 1996, and as we know from well-documented experience, a road-building plan is about as reliable as a railway timetable. The "purple route" was approved as far back as January 1988. In 1992 it was re-examined and changes, including a dual carriageway, were proposed. A revised lay-out was submitted for approval in October 1993. Then there were more objections and a further revised lay-out was finally approved by the highways sub-committee in October 1994. One encouraging factor is that the scheme is on the priority list for those costing over £2 million.

The five-kilometre link starts from the Harden Park roundabout and stretches via Brook Lane across land to a new roundabout to link with the Chelford Road roundabout. Then it crosses the railway and Welsh Row before finally rejoining the A34 near Alderley Park. While all this will mean better air quality in the village by diverting well over 2,000 cars

an hour at peak times, those living near the route will have less cause to rejoice. Members of Alderley Edge golf club may well find themselves with a new tee and green; an equestrian centre faces relocation and eight rights of way could be severed. It is expected that a farm will be demolished, eleven others will probably lose land and another seven will have access problems.

An official report says several properties "would initially experience high visual intrusion until the proposed landscape planting becomes fully established. Twelve properties may be eligible for noise insulation and some 94 properties may experience a perceptible increase in noise levels." The consolation for all this is an anticipated reduction of traffic, not only in the village, but also of 75 per cent in Nether Alderley and 65 per cent in Ryleys Lane.

It seems unlikely that Alderley Edge, with its own cosy, comfortable, and non-cosmopolitan identity will suffer much loss of trade to the out-of-town developments. Wilmslow and Handforth most certainly will. Whether Wilmslow will survive as the flourishing town we have all grown to enjoy and appreciate, is debatable. Perhaps there is encouragement to be learned from a very small town called Northleach, in the Cotswolds, where dense high-street traffic made life hell for the townsfolk. Overnight, traders lost 20 per cent of their turnover when the by-pass opened. The anti-bypass prophets of doom seemed to have been proved right. But then visitors and tourists started recognising and appreciating the new-found peace and tranquillity and began to return. Today, Northleach is thriving better than ever before.

Survival for Wilmslow depends on how much united effort community leaders, councillors and tradespeople are prepared to make to overcome the many problems. It will be a long, uphill struggle.

GOLF COURSES OF CHESHIRE

Mark Rowlinson (£9.95)

"Reminders of how many treasures have still to be visited" **Daily Telegraph**

This is a comprehensive guide to over 80 of Cheshire's golf courses. Includes detailed descriptions, clear two-colour maps and a card for each course.

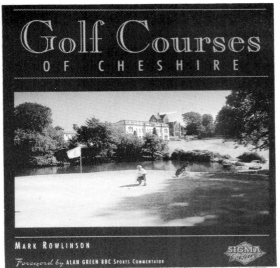

More local interest books from Sigma . . .

GOLDEN DAYS: a Macclesfield Life – Paul Maybury (£6.95)

PORTRAIT OF MACCLESFIELD – Doug Pickford (£6.95)

MACCLESFIELD, SO WELL REMEMBERED – Doug Pickford (£6.95)

MACCLESFIELD, THOSE WERE THE DAYS – Doug Pickford (£6.95)

PORTRAIT OF STOCKPORT – John Creighton (£6.95)

PORTRAIT OF MANCHESTER – John Creighton (£6.95)

MACCLESFIELD IN PICTURES & POEMS

Dorothy Bentley Smith (£9.95)

This delightful book explores the history of Macclesfield in a unique way: the visual interest of both old and new photographs is set against entertaining and thought-provoking poetry. The book is written by a respected local historian and is an ideal introduction to the town for visitors and Maxonians, both young and old.

Myths, Legends & Folklore:

SHADOWS: A NORTHERN INVESTIGATION OF THE UNKNOWN – Steve Cliffe (£7.95)

DARK TALES OF OLD CHESHIRE – Angela Conway (£6.95)

CHESHIRE: ITS MAGIC & MYSTERY – Doug Pickford (£7.95)

MYTHS AND LEGENDS OF EAST CHESHIRE – Doug Pickford (£5.95)

SUPERNATURAL STOCKPORT – Martin Mills (£5.95)

CHILLING TRUE TALES OF OLD LANCASHIRE – Keith Johnson (£7.95)

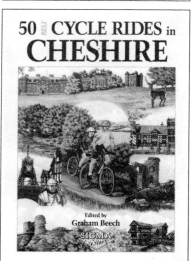

Country Walking – Cheshire & The Peak District

TEA SHOP WALKS IN CHESHIRE – Clive Price *(£6.95)*

TEA SHOP WALKS IN THE PEAK DISTRICT – Norman & June Buckley *(£6.95)*

HALF DAY WALKS IN THE PEAK DISTRICT – Alan Bradley *(£6.95)*

PEAKLAND RIVER VALLEY WALKS – Tony Stephens *(£7.95)*

BEST PUB WALKS: CHESTER & THE DEE VALLEY – John Haywood *(£6.95)*

EAST CHESHIRE WALKS – Graham Beech *(£5.95)*

WEST CHESHIRE WALKS – Jen Darling *(£5.95)*

RAMBLES AROUND MANCHESTER – Mike Cresswell *(£6.95)*

PUB WALKS IN CHESHIRE – Jen Darling *(£6.95)*

NW WATERWAY WALKS: SOUTH OF THE MERSEY – Guy Lawson *(£6.95)*

NW WATERWAY WALKS: THE MERSEY WATERWAYS – David Parry *(£6.95)*

Cycling . . .

CYCLE UK! The essential guide to leisure cycling – Les Lumsdon *(£9.95)*

OFF-BEAT CYCLING IN THE PEAK DISTRICT – Clive Smith *(£6.95)*

50 BEST CYCLE RIDES IN CHESHIRE – Graham Beech *(£7.95)*

Sport . . .

RED FEVER: from Rochdale to Rio as 'United' supporters – Steve Donoghue *(£7.95)*

DESPATCHES FROM OLD TRAFFORD – Richard Kurt *(£6.95)*

UNITED WE STOOD: unofficial history of the Ferguson years – Richard Kurt *(£6.95)*

MANCHESTER CITY: Moments to Remember – John Creighton *(£9.95)*

AN A-Z OF MANCHESTER CITY – Dean Hayes *(£6.95)*

STEAM MOTIVE POWER CENTRES

No. 51: SOUTH AFRICA

A Colour Pictorial — Compiled by Roger Griffiths

INTRODUCTION PAGE

Keith Pirt visited South Africa five times, in the winter months of 1980 – 1984. This was rather late on in steam days in the Republic, because compared with only a year or two before, traction modernisation had considerably limited the locations where steam could be seen in any quantity and also, the variety of locomotive classes on offer. Nevertheless, Keith Pirt's unsurpassed skills with a camera and perfect eye for a location, coupled to the South African winter's unmatched conditions of cold, clear skies and low angle sun, ensured that whatever steam action was to be seen, he captured it in all its glory! Your author has been familiar with the railways of Southern Africa since the early 1970s and it is a great pleasure to bring to you some of The Master's work from his visits there.

Roger Griffiths, Cyprus, 2009

(Cover) **Loco 26 3450, 4-8-4 L.D.Porta and a Class GMAM Garratt 4-8-2+2-8-4, are seen near Perdeburg on the Kimberley to Bloemfontein line, with a dynamometer car test train, comprising a 1800-ton freight load. August 1983.** *KRP C325*

(Title Page) **Another dynamometer car test train for 26 3450, as she heads a lengthy freight from Bloemfontein to Kimberley. However, she has help from a Class GMAM Garratt that had been included in the 1800 tonne train as a mixture of extra dead-weight (the Garratt not working), and brake power (not to mention giving wonderful photo opportunities to the veritable squadron of cars chasing the train)! As an example of such opportunities, the early morning sun of August 1983 allows a classic back-lit "glint" shot, as the train rounds the 90 degree curve on the approach to Perdeburg station.** *KRP C326*

Printed and bound by The Amadeus Press, Cleckheaton, West Yorkshire

First published in the United Kingdom by Book Law Publications, 382 Carlton Hill, Nottingham, NG4 1JA

SAR, Cape Northern System:
Mafeking – Vryburg – Warrenton – Kimberley line

Prior to 1980 this route was worked in two distinct sections: Mafeking to Vryburg traffic was hauled by Class 19D 4-8-2 and on, from Vryburg to Warrenton Class 25NC 4-8-4 held sway. From Warrenton to Kimberley the line was electrified, but steam worked over it nevertheless. But, there was a traction problem - though very capable engines, the 19Ds were proving not up to the demands of the large traffic passing through Mafeking to and from Rhodesia/Zimbabwe and Zambia. To ease the situation, the first Class GMA/M Garratt arrived at Mafeking late in 1980 and the type quickly supplanted the 19Ds on heavy line work, with the smaller engines then handling shunting and lighter duties. The GMA/Ms' reign was brief though, as Class 25NC 4-8-4 took over line work throughout, from 1984.
Mafeking engine shed is seen here in August 1983, when it was serving as the last bastion of Garratt operation on the SAR. This picture is made more interesting because just seen in the background are the distinctive smoke deflectors mounted each side of the chimney of 19D 2644. Built by Krupp (1824/1938), that machine had been modified in 1978, by Briton David Wardale, with some features a la Dante Porta, the Argentinean steam "wizard". 2644 then served as a test bed for some of the ideas later incorporated in the massive 1979/81 rebuilding of 4-8-4 25NC 3450, which became 26 3450 L.D.Porta. *KRP C720*

3

Class 19D 2705 (Borsig 14756/1939), leaves Mareetsane with a stopping passenger train from Vryburg to Mafeking, in August 1983. The Class 19 series of locomotives was one of the most successful designs ever to run on the SAR, being found literally everywhere on the system. Weighing-in at around 80 tons plus tender, these 4-8-2s had two, 21" x 26" cylinders, 200psi boiler pressure and 4'-6" wheels, giving a tractive effort at 75% pressure (the SAR's preferred measure, against the 85% used in say, (UK), of 31,850 pounds. *KRP C478*

The line between Mafeking and Vryburg was scenically, not one of the best, being generally straight and gently undulating. One of the best locations, however, could be found at Kraaipan, where southbound trains traversed a 90 degree curve, with interesting background detail and small, trees that could be used for framing the subject. Garratt GMAM 4085 (BP 7751/1955), heads a freight to Vryburg, in the late afternoon's setting sun. August 1983. *KRP C719*

5

Earlier in the day at Kraaipan, Keith Pirt captured this classic Garratt-esque broadside shot of GMAM 4065 (Hen 28694/1954), as it headed north with a freight for Mafeking. Another most successful design, if a bit heavy on maintenance, these 191 ton locomotives were specifically designed as a "double 19D". As such they featured slightly smaller diameter cylinders - four at 20½ "x 26" - 200psi pressure, 4'-6" wheels and a massive 60,700 pounds of tractive effort! *KRP C480*

The cold, crisp early morning air and brilliant sunshine provide a wonderfully back-lit shot of the daily 0630 stopping passenger train from Mafeking to Vryburg, near Vryhof. The pairing of articulated and non-articulated locomotive types was uncommon, so it is assumed that GMAM 4080 (BP 7554/1954), was piloting the usual Class 19D - here a "torpedo" tender version, No. 3356 (NBL 26076/1948) - on a balancing turn. That's a lot of horsepower for just 10 coaches! August 1983. *KRP C477*

Prior to 1984, Mafeking 19D and GMAM locos used to hand over at Vryburg to 25NC Class 4-8-4, for the journey south to Warrenton. Following track upgrading works the big 4-8-4s started making inroads into the traffic north of Vryburg, eventually supplanting the GMAM. Early in that change in motive power, near Kameel, an unidentified 25NC (actually a rebuild of a Class 25 Condenser), roars north with a freight from Vryburg, in characteristic 25NC fashion. May 1984. *KRP C800*

Jan Kempdorf station in August 1980, as an unidentified Class 25NC passes through with a freight from Vryburg to Warrenton. The 4-8-4 is proceeding slowly because of track works, attended by a pair of Class 19Ds on permanent way trains. The 25NCs working this route were based at Beaconsfield depot, Kimberley, out-stationed at Warrenton. *KRP C1024*

Before leaving the Cape Northern district, a look at a typical large steam shed in the midst of electrified territory. Klerksdorp is situated halfway between Johannesburg and Warrenton, serving a network of branch lines to the north and west, as well as a major cross-country route south, to Kroonstad, in the Orange Free State. By August 1980, when this picture was taken, only shunting and light turns remained for Klerksdorp shed's steam locos. Several 19Ds are visible together with a single Class 25NC, which doubtless had worked up from Warrenton. *KRP C555*

SAR Cape Northern System: Kimberley – De Aar line

Legions of railway photographers visited the Kimberley – De Aar line to see a steam spectacle then like no other in the world, even China. Heavy traffic worked flat-out by huge locomotives – in other words - what it was ALL about! The South Africans too realised what a special line this was so they christened it the "Steel Kyalami", in an allusion to the Republic's premier Grand Prix circuit. Now that many years have passed since the end of steam it is safe to reveal that although the route's resident 25NC Class was officially limited to a maximum speed of 55 mph, it was not uncommon for that figure to daily be exceeded by anything up to 20 mph! Some of the enginemen responsible for such performances were latter-day Ken Hooles - expatriate Britons who moved to South Africa specifically to work on steam locomotives, after they had become extinct in their own country.

One of the favourite "phot-spots" was "The Horn", a raised location north of the bridge over the Orange River. All trains stopped at Orange River for fire-cleaning and water, resulting in a spectacle as the locomotives re-started their journey by climbing heavily away in both directions. Here 25NC 3523, built as a Class 25 Condenser (NBL 27383/1954), and converted to non-condensing form in the 1970s, lifts coal empties towards Kimberley and the Transvaal. August 1983. *KRP C474*

A classic photograph in every sense! Having earlier cleared some brushwood off the line, 25NC 3430 (Hen 28749/1953), positively
12 blisters past the isolated station of Poupan with the northbound Orange Express in August 1980. *KRP C467*

Seen near Poupan in super-shine condition, De Aar shed's 25NC 3436 Molly (Hen 28755/1953), hauls the daily, northbound De-Aar – Kimberley passenger train, in May 1984. The locomotive is named in typical De Aar fashion, after a female who was in some way, special to the loco's allocated driver. Seen to good effect is the dirt road that paralleled the line for most of the distance between Kimberley and De Aar. Your author well   remembers the epic chases by car-borne, camera-toting enthusiasts as they had to drive literally flat-out to get ahead of single and double-headed 25NCs, being driven equally flat-out! Oh, those potholes and sometimes, airborne progress by the car. *KRP C712*   13

In the early 1970s, De Aar shed was renowned for its museum of rare locomotive types, of 3'-6" and 2'-0" gauges, built up by the then depot foreman, Mr Watson, Then in 1976, the entire class of 25 GO Garratts – loco numbers 2572 to 2596 - came to De Aar for storage in the dry desert air. This was because of the dieselisation of the route that this smaller version of the Class GMA/M had monopolised since delivery from Henschel, in 1954 (Works Nos: 28705 – 29) - the Belfast to Steelport branch, in the SAR's Eastern Transvaal System. Based at Lydenburg shed, halfway along the branch, the GOs faced gradients of up to 1 in 33 as they lifted ore trains through no less than 4,444 feet, from Spekboom, to the line's 6,871 foot summit at Nederhorst, the highest point on SAR and a place frequently subject to blizzard conditions in South Africa's winter months. Indeed, so hard were the GOs worked that it was a routine matter for their petticoat pipes to be replaced every 14 days because of char cutting! By the time Keith Pirt visited De Aar depot in August 1980, the stored GOs had been reduced to just these eight examples. GO 2575 survives today (2008), but she is not in working condition. *KRP C464*

The sole surviving Class 25 Condenser is seen at De Aar shed in August 1983. The 25s were built to a design by Henschel, following that firm's experience with providing condensing locomotives for the Deutsche Reichsbahn during WW2, when the DR faced the arid conditions of Russia, following Hitler's invasion of the Soviet Union. Actually though, Henschel built only the first Class 25 – No. 3451 – (28730/1953), sending it to North British, which company delivered the remaining 89 locomotives – 3452 to 3540 – during 1953/4 (Works Nos. 27312 – 400). Despite previous experience with condensing locomotives, the Class 25 was subject to considerable teething troubles, mainly with the exhaust fan in the smokebox, which gave these engines their unique, jet-engine whine. Once such problems were overcome, these huge machines – the engine portion weighed over 120 tons, while the tender, which was longer, scaled almost 114 tons – settled down to very successful service, with savings of up to 85% in water consumption being achieved. They were expensive to maintain though, so as soon as the desert lines they worked were put under diesel or electric haulage, 89 condensers were very successfully rebuilt to Class 25NC standards. *KRP C619*

15

Specially hauling a train for the visit to the De Aar – Kimberley line by the Cape Town branch of the Railway Society of South Africa, 25 3511 whines north from De Aar with a lengthy freight. The distant Koppie (mountain) near Behrshoek, formed a background to innumerable enthusiasts' pictures! August 1983. *KRP C343*

16

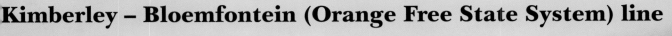

SAR Cape Northern System:
Kimberley – Bloemfontein (Orange Free State System) line

The line from Kimberley to Bloemfontein had several very popular photographic locations. Probably the premier spot was just east of Perdeburg station where the Modder River is traversed by a simple plate girder bridge allowing a great, low-angle shot of locos making the crossing. Here Class 25NC 3472, another condenser rebuild (origin NBL 27332/1953), has steam to spare as she crosses the river, depleted as always, during South Africa's dry winter months; August 1983. Your author visited this spot on one occasion with several fellow enthusiasts, to find the location untenable, due to the presence of a large, but seemingly, benign Cape Cobra! We did nothing to disturb its peaceful demeanour, thereby living to phot another day! *KRP C773*

The staff at many SAR stations diligently followed the tradition laid down in Britain, of maintaining their stations and especially, the gardens, in immaculate condition. Here we see a typical example, at Immigrant station, with its perfectly gravelled platform, manicured lawns and a wonderful flower bed featuring cacti, aloe plants and Nqama daisies. Waiting in the station with a Kimberley – Bloemfontein freight, is Class 15F 4-8-2 3081 (NBL 25965/1948), while 25NC 3498 (NBL 27359/1954 – built as Class 25), clears the single line with a freight for Bloemfontein. The picture dates from August 1983 and the author is sad to reflect that during his last extensive visit to the SAR, in July 1999, no such care was being given to any station's appearance, anywhere. *KRP C344*

Another favourite spot for photographers was Bloemfontein Showgrounds, where a less than exciting background was more than compensated for by nice curves and good sun for most of the day. 25NC3475 (NBL 27335/1953 – as Class 25) has just left Bloemfontein station with the Orange Express, bound for Kimberley in August 1983. *KRP C620*

With its severely graded, sinuous route through dramatic scenery, the Bloemfontein to Bethlehem line was second only to De Aar – Kimberly in attracting railway photographers, so your author makes no excuse for exhibiting ten of Keith Pirt's pictures featuring the line. It is sobering to reflect, however, that today (2008), there is no regular traffic whatsoever over the full distance between Bloemfontein and Bethlehem!

There were only three lines diverging from the Bloemfontein to Bethlehem route; the first reached from Bloemfontein, was at Sannaspos, where a long, meandering secondary line ran south to Burgersdorp, that line today having effectively been "mothballed" since the 1990s. Next came the station of Marseilles, from where a very scenic and heavily graded branch ran across the border to Maseru, capital of the mountainous Kingdom of Lesotho. This route was very busy in steam days, with traffic in the care of 19D 4-8-2, many trains having to be banked by a second 19D for the first few miles out of Marseilles. Such assistance, however, was not being given when Keith Pirt visited in August 1980, and captured 19D 2767 (RSH 2780/1945), working hard upgrade, with the mid-day "international" mixed, having just left Marseilles. *KRP C511*

The third place where a line branches off is at Modderpoort, junction for the short line to Ladybrand. Modderpoort also served as a sub-shed of Bloemfontein depot, being at roughly the half-way point between there and Bethlehem. This was the turn-round point for daily pick-up freights that ran from both ends of the line, their locomotives laying-over at Modderpoort before making their return runs. Each lunchtime then, three engines would be seen on the sub-shed's roads (there was no building): in the early 1980s these were usually a 25NC from Bethlehem, a 15F from Bloemfontein and a 19D, or on occasion, a venerable Class 15AR 4-8-2, for the Ladybrand shuttle service. Very early one August morning in 1983, Keith Pirt stationed himself a few miles west of Modderpoort and timed it almost to perfection as the rising sun's rays are just high enough to catch 15F 2960 (NBL 24500/1939), hammering up the stiff climb witha pick-up freight for Bloemfontein. *KRP C626*

21

Seen leaving the delightful little township of Ladybrand with the morning freight for Modderpoort, was this 19D 4-8-2. Keith Pirt's notes do not identify the locomotive, but they do reveal that it carried a number in the 3321 to 3370 series, the last batch of 19D, delivered in 1949 by North British. As such they were built with the 6,500 gallon/12 tons coal capacity "torpedo" tenders, and Keith notes that this particular 19D had lost that in favour of an earlier design of tender. He also recognises that the engine is working boiler-first, the opposite of normal practice for traffic out of Ladybrand and moreover, that the "freight" does not deserve that appellation, being comprised as it was of a single guard's compartment brake! August 1983. *KRP C337*

With a line abounding in great photo locations, picking the best is difficult. However, one of your author's favourites was from high up on the side of a Koppie, looking down into the Owanti Gorge, where the railway went through a dramatic S-bend as it climbed westwards, out of the gorge. As such it was first class for moving and still photos, as amply demonstrated here, with 25NC 3419 (Hen 28738/1953), battling up the gradient with, nevertheless, steam to spare. The train was the daily Bethlehem to Bloemfontein passenger service, the date: August 1983. *KRP C615*

Another place on the Bloemfontein to Bethlehem line where, even in the middle of nowhere, you could hardly place a foot without stepping on a discarded film packet, was Sekonyela! It is obvious why, with that very prominent Koppie which formed the background to legions of photos of trains heading east. As here, when in August 1984, Keith Pirt waited until just the right moment and the smoke from the unidentified 25NC hauling the Bloemfontein to Bethlehem passenger, had nicely framed the rock formation. Your scribe camped overnight here in 1980, vividly recalling Stephen Spielberg's Close Encounters of the Third Kind, and waiting, in vain, for the aliens' mother ship to appear from behind the Koppie! *KRP C998*

With an enormous plume of black smoke telling of a mechanical stoker working overtime, 25NC 3411 (NBL 27296/1953,) was going flat-out in July 1982, as she brought a Bloemfontein to Bethlehem passenger up the heavy grade, to the enigmatically named station of Generaalsnek. *KRP C616*

25

Fouriesburg was another place where the twisting route of the line allowed photo locations to move more or less throughout the day, as the sun crossed the sky. Best, however, was literally just off the station end, going west, and for a mile or so beyond that, as the line climbed heavily through a series of S-curves. Here, 25NC 3413 (Hen 28732/1953), pulls away from a Fouriesburg stop with the morning pick-up freight from Bethlehem to Modderpoort. August 1982. *KRP C470*

Twenty one months after the previous picture was taken and some hundreds of yards further west, Keith Pirt had made another very early morning start and perfectly positioned himself again to catch the first rays of the morning sun. This time they illuminate an uncommon double-heading of Class 25NC, as leaving Fouriesburg, they lift a superb smoke trail in the sky. Nos.3403 and 3410 (NBL 27288 and 27295/1953, respectively), were hauling a "Bombela", or "Native" train, from Bethlehem to Ficksburg. Such special trains were run by SAR at public holiday times – in this instance, for South Africa's (then) Republic Day. *KRP C340*

During South Africa's dry winters, the supply of water became problematical, especially along the eastern end of the Bloemfontein to Bethlehem route. Accordingly, SAR ran special trains of water tank wagons, for delivery at various central locations. Just such a Bethlehem- bound train is seen here, nearing Ionia Summit, hauled by an unidentified 25NC. It is August 1983 and the winter must have been mild hereabouts: look at the trees in blossom and in the far distance, above the 3rd, 4th and 5th tank cars, a splash of purple on the hillside. That will be Jacaranda trees in flower – something not normally seen until September/October. *KRP C621*

Bethlehem locomotive shed on a sunny morning in August 1980. Three workers pause in the work of preparing 25NC 3410 for her next job. The locomotive carries the unofficial name Bethlehem on her smoke deflectors and the trademark, diamond-shaped works plate of the North British Locomotive Company – in this instance, carrying the builder's number and date: 27295, of 1953. *KRP C702*

SAR Cape Eastern System: Queenstown – Burgersdorp line

The main line from East London to Springfontein was dieselised in the early 1970s, but the northern end particularly, still saw considerable local steam working into the 1980s. Locomotives were based at Queenstown shed, with sub-depots at Sterkstroom and Burgersdorp. Some of the motive power was provided by the aged, but very popular and capable, Class 15AR 4-8-2, two of which are seen here, in August 1982, near Stormberg, climbing strongly with a freight to Burgersdorp. Loco Nos. 2100 and 1820 were built as Class 15A, (NBL 21729/1920 and Maf 5645/1925, respectively), and 2100 is of particular interest as she was delivered experimentally equipped with Lentz poppet valves, but they were soon replaced by standard Walschaerts valve gear and piston valves. The poppet valves made a come-back however, with the later SAR classes, 4-8-2 15E, 4-6-2 16E and 4-8-2 19C. *KRP C456*

SAR Cape Eastern System: Schoombee – Hofmeyr branch

The secondary line from Stormberg to Rosmead had one branch line, that from Schoombee to Hofmeyr, which saw one, weekdays only mixed train each way, handled by Class 24 2-8-4 from Rosmead depot. Here we see the last Class 24 built, No. 3700 (NBL 26412/1949) taking water at Schoombee, after arriving with a mixed from Hofmeyr. August 1982. *KRP C459*

SAR Cape Eastern System: Sterkstroom – Maclear Branch

At well over 100 miles in length it is hardly right to describe the heavily graded and sinuous line from Sterkstroom to Maclear as a "branch"! Staple motive power was the Class 19D 4-8-2 which had to be worked very hard, with some double-heading necessary on the heavier trains. Amid dramatic scenery, 19D 2740 (RSH 7253/1945), climbs away from Birds River with a morning freight from Sterkstroom to Maclear.

August 1982. *KRP C710*

A maximum effort is evident as 19Ds 2712 and 2741 (Borsig 14763/1939 and RSH 7254/1945, respectively), climb towards Glen Wallace station with a Maclear to Sterkstroom train. Despite the work being done, however, there is still steam to spare – evidence of the excellent locomotive design that was the 19D. *KRP C613*

More scenic majesty on the Strekstroom to Maclear branch! A scarcely populated, mountainous backdrop is provided for a Class 19D topping Penhoek summit with a passenger train for Maclear, in August 1982. Although unidentified by Keith Pirt, the locomotive was almost certainly numbered in the 27xx series, as that batch of engines, mostly supplied by Robert Stephenson & Hawthorn in 1945, monopolised workings on this particular line. *KRP C333*

A 19D, number not known, climbs through the S-bends after leaving Dordecht in August 1980, with a short freight from Maclear to Sterkstroom. The locomotive is worthy of comment because it obviously has a regular crew that spend time keeping it in immaculate condition . Note the silvered chimney, running plate edge and wheel rims, the latter also having red-painted centres, and the white-painted cow-catcher. See also that the crew has added some very non-standard smoke deflectors (hardly effective no doubt), with red-painted inner surfaces. Lastly, the engine has a subsidiary water tank, again a non-standard feature for the 19D class, except in the Cape Eastern System, with its generally arid terrain. *KRP C707*

The setting sun casts a pinkish glow over the smoke from a Class 15AR 4-8-2, passing Bailey station with a freight from Queenstown to Sterkstroom, in August 1980. Note that the loco carries a signature decoration of Queenstown depot – the white-rimmed wheels with red balance weights. Again, Keith Pirt only identifies the locomotive as being numbered in the 2011 to 2100 series, supplied as Class 15A in two batches: 2011 - 2025 from North British in 1921 (Works Nos. 22736 – 50), and 2008 - 2100 from Maffei in 1925 (5625 – 45). As alluded to earlier, these engines were highly thought of and can credit their long lives to the fact that they simply were a great design – probably the finest by D.A.Hendrie, who was Chief Mechanical Engineer to South African Railways, from its formation in 1910, to 1922. *KRP C791*

Queenstown's spaciously laid out, eight-road locomotive depot is depicted here in August 1980. Engines of classes 15AR, 19D and 24 are to be seen, of which the immaculate 15AR is worthy of note, with its yellow-painted reversing lever and Queenstown's white-rimmed wheels, the latter also seen on the distant Class 24 2-8-4. The overhead coaling gantry, so typical of SAR steam sheds, has been given a fresh coat of primer as part of a repaint. Now, if this had been a depot in late British Railways days, such a repaint would probably presaged imminent closure of the shed! Queenstown, however, continued in steam service at least until 1983 and stands today (2008, hosting a dump of over 25 steam locos. *KRP C789*

SAR Cape Eastern System: Imvani – Qamata branch

The Imvani – Qamata branch was another tortuous line trailing off into the dry Cape Eastern mountains. The route was not as lengthy as the Maclear branch some 50 miles north, but traffic was buoyant, with morning and afternoon mixed trains that ran to and from Queenstown. Here we see 19D 2726 (RSH 7196/1945) making an energetic start from Qamata with the afternoon mixed in August 1982. Keith Pirt's records comment that the train was made more interesting by the two, ex-works clerestory-roofed coaches at the rear – a total of four passenger vehicles, indicating a healthy amount of traffic. *KRP C617*

In August 1982 Keith Pirt visited the Fort Beaufort – Seymour line which branches off the Blaney to Cookhouse secondary main line. Locomotive power for the daily return mixed was the ubiquitous 19D based at East London shed, out-stationed at Adelaide. Passing a nicely treed, un-named wayside halt, we see 19D 2631 (Skoda 946/1938) with the mixed from Fort Beaufort to Seymour. *KRP C643*

Later in the same day as the previous picture, 19D 2631 is seen crossing a river bridge near Upsher, on the return run to Fort Beaufort. South Africa's peerless clear atmosphere allows a view into the far distance of this remote area, with its branch line that was something of a time-warp, passing through places where things moved somewhat slowly. The train's make-up reflects this with aged and by then rare, non-bogie livestock vans and low-sided open wagons. *KRP C564*

Of all the branches in the Cape district the Alicedale – Grahamstown – Port Alfred line was perhaps the biggest magnet for enthusiasts. The route abounded in sharp curves, fierce gradients, tunnels, a spectacular bridge or two, all in magnificent scenery and generally, not difficult to access from nearby dirt roads. In your author's opinion the best section of all was that from Grahamstown to the delightful town of Port Alfred, but tragically that portion was totally closed in the latter 1990s. In happier times though, traffic over all the line was buoyant and heavy so the resident 19Ds had to be worked very hard, with considerable double- heading. Here 19D 2736 (NBL 7249/1945), clears Tunnel No.1 with the afternoon Alicedale to Grahamstown freight, which included two ex- works passenger coaches in its make-up. The fireman takes a short break from his many labours and watches the scenery drift past. July 1983. *KRP C993*

One of the best photo locations for trains travelling from Grahamstown to Alicedale, was the S-bends on the heavy climb to Highlands station. 19D 3326 (with short tender) and 2751 (NBL 26046/1948 and RSH 7264/1945, respectively), put out a maximum effort as they lift their afternoon freight towards the summit. August 1983. *KRP C463*

As Keith Pirt says in his notes "a different view", from August 1983. It is atmospheric too, as a pair of 19Ds roll into Grahamstown station with the afternoon passenger train from Alicedale, which also featured a brace of refrigerator vans behind the locos. A third 19D is seen running through the station to back onto the train for Alicedale, just seen at right. There is something faintly "British" about this scene, with the lattice footbridge, canopied station platforms with their flower pots, a prospective passenger wheeling a bicycle and the porter's trolley, standing waiting a "tipping" client. *KRP C930*

43

Locomotive operations on the Alicedale to Port Alfred branch were centred upon this 3-road shed at Grahamstown, seen in August 1983, with six 19Ds visible, the locomotives being out-stationed from Port Elizabeth's Sydenham shed. It is evident that Grahamstown depot is a relatively new structure – indeed, it had replaced a much older and dilapidated building about 1970. Continuing the "British-ness" alluded to above, the shed has a coaling tower that would not have been out of place anywhere in UK, but such a design was very unusual on SAR. In addition, because of limited space, the depot could not feature the usual locomotive-turning triangle; instead it was equipped with a turntable that was sited behind the photographer, close-by the station. This too was a very rare feature for the SAR. Your scribe has just consulted "Google, Earth" for Grahamstown and in an image dated 2008, it can be seen that the engine shed and turntable still exist, but all tracks leading to them have been lifted. *KRP C799*

SAR Cape Midland System: The Port Elizabeth area

The 4-track main line from Port Elizabeth to Swartkops was a total magnet for enthusiasts with its intensive steam-worked suburban service: 11-coach trains covering 21 miles, with eight intermediate stops, in 50 minutes, called for really first class running! For your author's first visit in the early 1970s, Class 10BR Pacifics were in the process of being replaced by 16CR 4-6-2, then by 1976 the superb Class 15AR were in charge, all these types being supported by Classes 19D, 24 and GMAM Garratts on other services. By the early 1980s, only the Garratts were no longer to be seen; the 15ARs were still in charge of the suburban trains – and still in the immaculate condition that was Port Elizabeth, Sydenham shed's trademark.

Locomotives aplenty in this August 1980 view of Sydenham's eight-road shed. Just two classes can be identified – a very clean 15AR among lots of Class 12R 4-8-2, the staple shunting power for Port Elizabeth's docks and extensive freight yards. *KRP C503*

Swartkops Junction was where the 4-track section ended and two routes diverged. Westwards went the line via Uitenhage, Oudtshoorn, the Montague Pass and the "Garden Route" to eventually reach Cape Town. Eastwards went the main line to Alicedale (and on to De Aar), off which came the branches to Alexandria and Kirkwood. Approaching Swartkops from Uitenhage the line crossed a wetland that was a favourite place for photographers, including Keith Pirt. An unidentified Class 15AR heads a morning local train to Port Elizabeth, in August 1980. *KRP C504*

The large Swartkops Power Station adds to the exhaust coming from an unidentified Class 24 2-8-4, as it takes the Alicedale line at Swartkops Junction, in August 1980. The locomotive is hauling a very varied set of vehicles in the morning mixed train that will eventually traverse the branch line to Alexandria – two modern container flats followed by two old, 4-wheel wagons are noteworthy. Like virtually all large "industrial" locations throughout South Africa, Swartkops Power Station once had its own 3'-6" gauge steam shunting locomotive. That was an 0-4-0ST built by Robert Stephenson & Hawthorn, that happily survived and today resides in the railway museum at Outeniqua. *KRP C506* 47

A mile or so further along the Alicedale line from Swartkops Junction and nearing the summit of a severe climb is 19D 3339, with an August 1980, afternoon train for the Kirkwood branch. No. 3339 was the regular locomotive for that branch, with a regular crew, who were obviously aware that a cameraman was about! It is equally obvious that the same crew spent a lot of time embellishing "their" engine with brass decorations and keeping the whole machine in a beautiful condition. Despite having the 6,500 gallon "torpedo" tender with which 3339 was built (NBL 26059/1948), the scarcity of water along her daily route has made it necessary for the loco to haul a subsidiary water tank. *KRP C462*

The spick and span little town of Despatch witnesses 15AR 2017 (NBL 22742/1921), make a spirited departure with a Saturday morning, 12- coach local train from Uitenhage to Port Elizabeth, in August 1982. The engine was at that time, out-stationed at Uitenhage and carries that shed's legendary cleanliness – perhaps even better than that achieved at Sydenham! It is sad to reflect that such esprit de corps is today, very seldom found on the "modern" railway, virtually anywhere in the world. *KRP C334*

Despatch station again, this time northward, in August 1980, as a pair of nicely clean, Class 15AR pass a typical bracket signal, with what Keith Pirt described as a "lengthy" freight for Uitenhage. The locomotives' identities were not noted. *KRP C1022*

Bowling along in fine style at Redhouse, was this unknown Class 15AR with a freight from Port Elizabeth to Uitenhage, in August 1980. The train is composed almost entirely of loaded coal wagons from the Transvaal and bound, no doubt, for Uitenhage locomotive shed and on, to such depots as Kliplaat and Oudtshoorn etc. Thus exposed is one of the steam locomotive's Achilles' Heels – the necessity of burning fuel to get further fuel to places that have no indigenous supplies. A big bonus with this train though was the Class NG15, a 2'-0" gauge 2-8-2 and tender, destined for overhaul at Uitenhage Works. This type was nicknamed "Kalahari" from its original introduction on the now defunct 2'-0" gauge lines in South West Africa – today's Namibia. By the 1960s, however, the NG15 worked exclusively on the 2'-0" lines that ran west from Port Elizabeth, for no less than 177 miles to Avontuur! This particular NG15 would have been transferred to the 3'-6" gauge low flat in the 2'-0"/3'-6" transhipment yard at Port Elizabeth, Humewood Road. *KRP C995*

The afternoon sun beautifully back-lights the exhaust from 24 3665 (NBL 26377/1949), as she approaches the terminus at Somerset East with the daily mixed train. The 2-8-4 will then shunt the station yard, form up the return train and depart, to arrive back at Cookhouse in the evening. This was a pattern of service that had not changed for many years, but was inevitably destined soon to end with the increasing influence of road transport. *KRP C473*

South African industry centred round many, many mines, extracting a plethora of minerals, but mostly of course, coal, gold and platinum. Much of the coal would be burned in power stations that generated electricity to drive such things as paper mills, cement works, steel plants and even, one or two explosives factories. At the other end of the spectrum came the many sugar cane plantations and crushing mills of Natal, but all of these industrial concerns had a common feature – virtually every one had its own internal railway system, that could range from literally a few hundred yards of track, up to networks totalling scores of miles in length. Why, until it closed its doors in 1994, there was even a specialist company - Dunns Locomotive Works, at Witbank - that purchased locomotives second-hand from industrial lines, SAR – and even Rhodesian Railways – refurbished them and sold them on, or hired them, to industrial concerns. In this way enthusiasts were able to see many old, former "main line" classes still at work, something that was in itself a major attraction for all lovers of the steam locomotive. That was of course until the late 70s/early 80s, when companies started to close their railway systems and turn over to road transport or conveyor systems, which meant that many industrial lines disappeared in a relatively short period. By the time Keith Pirt started to visit South Africa there was indeed, still some very good quality industrial steam action to be seen, but it was concentrated on relatively few sites. Here are a few, all of which, however, have long since ceased operating steam.

Randfontein East Gold Mine (REGM)
REGM 4-8-0 No. 1 Trixie is seen on-shed at Randfontein East Mine, in August 1983. This locomotive was a former SAR Class 1, a type designed by D.A.Hendrie of the Natal Government Railway and introduced in 1904, with 71 examples being delivered by North British, in the years up to 1910. The locos featured a massive Belpaire boiler delivering saturated steam to Walschaerts-driven slide valve. What is significant about this type is that it formed a direct basis of development for later eight-coupled SAR types, of Classes 3, 12, 14, 15, 23 and 25. *KRP C623* 53

Another rare, ex-SAR class is seen at REGM's shed in August 1983 - a 4-8-2 of Class 15BR. This was basically a Canadian-built, bar-framed version of the numerous Class 15A, but only 30 15BR were delivered, as Class 15B: Nos. 1829 – 1838 and 1971 to 1990 (MLW 58440 – 49/1918 and 61424 – 43/1920, respectively). The class was taken out of service in the late 1970s, with one or two then finding their way into industrial use. *KRP C1028*

The SAR started to seriously rid itself of its last Garratts, the GMA/M, in the early 1980s but there was a market for some in industry and the REGM surprised more than a few people when it decided to purchase some GMA/M for hauling super-heavy ore trains from the loaders to the crushers. This was part of an expansion by REGM, which was planning to increase production by opening a new mine shaft. That opening occurred in August 1983 and Keith Pirt was on hand to witness it and photograph the unique, ceremonial passenger train provided for the guests and hauled by R9, one of REGM's newly acquired Garratts. Note the loco's very striking livery of an almost-Caledonian shade of blue. *KRP C624*

Nine months later Keith Pirt again visited Randfontein East Gold Mine and this time found another ex-SAR GMAM and train at the new mine shaft. R16 was in a very striking red livery with gold and black lining-out and was named Sarah. In fact all the locos working at REGM carried females' names, a la the De Aar tradition, to honour ladies special to the locomotives' crews. *KRP C1022*

Rustenburg Platinum Mine (RPM)

Up to the beginning of the 1970s, Rustenburg Platinum Mine's railway system was almost all of 2'-0" gauge, employing many aged, ex-SAR locomotives, including Garratts. There was also a short 3'-6" gauge section linking the mine to the SAR exchange sidings, worked by a solitary, huge 0-8-0T, a very rare industrial type for South Africa. By 1981, however, the 2 foot gauge was defunct and an extensive 3'-6" gauge system, totalling 70kms was in use, daily employing up to eight locomotives hauling ore ("reef" in local terms), from a number of shafts to the various processing plants. With a single exception, those engines came second-hand from the SAR and one of them is seen here, a former Class 14R 4-8-2, No. 1 Springbok, in green livery, seen at the mine's loco depot with a North British-built 4-8-4T No. 2. May 1984. *KRP C776*

RPM replaced its 0-8-0T with a 4-8-4T design in the early 1970s. That tank engine eventually went out of use for many years, but re-entered service in 1981, originally in a mixed, red, blue and green livery. By the time of Keith Pirt's visit in May/June 1984, however, the loco had been painted black, as seen here, as she shunts platinum reef wagons at the processing plant. North British provided the first of this very successful type of locomotive to South African industry in 1937 and between then and 1955, built over 50 examples in 4-8-4T and 4-8-2T form, plus a single 2-6-2T. In British parlance then, might they be described as South Africa's industrial "Black 5"? *KRP C631*

Black liveried RPM No. 3, an ex-SAR Class 14R, lifts 800 tonnes of platinum reef from the loader towards the processing plant in August 1983. The huge hills of tailings seen in the distance are a common sight around South Africa's mines and in fact, some of the earliest gold mine tailings heaps are today being re-processed, because the old extraction methods left amounts of gold that are today economically viable for exploitation. *KRP C991*

1000 tonnes of reef move from No. 6 shaft to the processor in May 1984, a journey of some miles and taken at quite high speed on RPM's superb track, which was maintained to main line standards. The locomotive is an ex-SAR Class 15CA 4-8-2, a type that grew to 84 examples during 1926- 1930, being built by Baldwin, Alco, Breda of Italy and North British. The 15CA was renowned as the "loudest" loco type on SAR, to which your scribe can attest, following a number of rides behind them in the early 70s. They were taken off main line use from the mid-1970s onwards, with a few then entering industrial service. *KRP C641*

The epitome of South African industrial steam operation, as still carrying its SAR number, RPM's red 14R 1754 (BP 5885/1915 – built as Class 14B), charges the bank on the approach to the Modder River bridge, with a 1000 tonne load of reef. August 1983. *KRP C483*

A few hundred yards further on from the previous picture, here is the RPM railway's bridge over the Modder River – the other Modder River, not to be confused with that crossed by SAR's Kimberley to De Aar main line. Casting a reflection in August 1983 was RPM No. 3, 62 ex-SAR 15CB 2071 (Baldwin 58717/1925). *KRP C782*

Rustenburg Platinum Mine's Frank Shaft is seen in the background as ex- SAR 14R 1756 (BP 5887/1915) smokes past with a 900 tonne train in May 1984. The picture was taken from a very prominent koppie that dominated the mine area and was visible for miles around. Your scribe has taken pictures from the self-same spot and well remembers that it was nicknamed "Kodak Heights"! *KRP C777*

63

Tavistock Colliery

The best evidence of a good locomotive design is its longevity in service. One such type was the SAR Class 11 2-8-2, designed by P.A.Hyde of the Central South African Railway; thirty six examples – SAR Nos. 912 to 947, being delivered by North British in 1903/4. After removal from main line work they rendered sterling service as shunters, only being withdrawn from the mid-1970s, with several moving on to industrial use. A pair of Class 11 went to Tavistock Colliery and here we have a fine portrait of No.2 resting in the sun, in its customary superb condition. The second Class 11 (TC No. 3) is visible behind. August 1983. *KRP C709*

Having delivered loaded wagons to the exchange sidings with the SAR and formed up a train of return empties Tavistock's No. 3 rolls back to the colliery in fine style, in August 1983. Note that the ex-Class 11 is running on superbly maintained track, something invariably far removed from similar railways in UK! *KRP C989*

Groot Vlei Proprietary Mines (GVPM)

Situated near Springs in the Transvaal, Groot Vlei Proprietary Mines' business was gold and platinum and like the Rustenburg Platinum Mine, GVPM had a sizeable internal railway system, but GVPM's speciality was the running of "Didos" – passenger trains taking the worker to the various shafts and processing plants. Like RPM, Groot Vlei also relied upon ex-SAR locomotives for its motive power, but unlike Rustenburg, the Groot Vlei stud was not nearly so "modern". Resident for many years was a trio of ex-SAR Class A 4-8-2T. The Class was significant because it was the first 4-8-2 design in the world and grew to no less than 100 examples, all coming from Dubs & Co., in the years 1888 – 1899. The Class A was replaced in the mid-1970s by a pair of these interesting engines. GVPM's descriptively named King Kong was an ex-SAR Class S 0-8-0 shunting engine, four of which came from Henschel in 1928/9. They proved so successful that they led to the S1 and S2 0-8-0 Classes, the first a massive design, the latter a much smaller type, 100 in number and having a great deal in common mechanically, with the contemporary Class 24 2-8-4. *KRP C992*

Joining the S Class at GVPM, in replacement of the Class A tanks, was a pair of ex-SAR Class 8DW 4-8-0. Another aged design, the Class 8 was introduced by H.M.Beatty of the Cape Government Railway, in 1902, with the 8D series being delivered by Neilson and North British in 1903. Originally un-superheated and equipped with slide valves, the SAR's CME, Mr A.G.Watson, had many of them rebuilt with straight- ported cylinders and long-travel piston valves (note the extended steam chest to accommodate the valve travel), with the re-classification to 8DW. Here we see GVPM's 8DW Puffing Duggie posing in the late afternoon sun at GVPM's gold mine section, in August 1983. *KRP C797*

GVPM's Puffing Duggie at work, propelling hoppers of gold reef to the processing plant, in August 1983. It is not exactly clear when this mine's veteran locomotives were finally retired, but rail operations ceased entirely in 1998. *KRP C330*

Class 26 4-8-4, No. 3450 L.D.Porta

To close this book it is appropriate to take a good look at what was a "great white hope" for the steam locomotive - the amazing rebuild of Class 25NC 3450 (Hen 28769/1953), incorporating many new design features, the brain child of Argentinean locomotive engineer, L. Dante Porta. The work was carried out under the supervision of a British disciple of Porta, David Wardale, who convinced the SAR management that he could produce a steam locomotive with greatly increased efficiency of operation. This would be realised through worthwhile savings in coal and water consumption and reduced preparation and disposal times, at a much cheaper unit cost than new diesel or electric locomotives. All this of course, was against South Africa's total lack of an oil resource, compared to the country's huge coal reserves, and at that time at least, a large and generally, semi-skilled labour force.

The rebuild was carried out at Salt River Works, Cape Town, but design work was spread throughout the SAR's various locomotive workshops. The primary objective was to improve combustion and steaming rate at the same time as reducing emission of black smoke, and to overcome the problem of clinkering. This was achieved by the use of a single-stage gas producer firebox. Additional major changes were the lengthening of the smokebox, provision of a double Lempor exhaust with offset double chimney and a feedwater-heater located between the chimneys. Redesigned valve liners incorporated streamlined ports to the cylinders, the rings and liners being made of very hard chromium cast iron. Improved lubrication techniques ensured that oil got to where it was most needed on the cylinder and valve liner rubbing surfaces, while other improvements were increased superheat, superheat booster, new piston valves, articulated valve spindles, new cooled valve liners, new cylinder liners, altered valve gear, Herdner starting valves, air sanding, altered self-cleaning smokebox, larger steam chests, direct steam pipes, improved pistons, improved valve and piston rod packings, variable stroke lubricator drive, improved insulation, and many minor detail changes.

The loco was first steamed in February 1981, soon moving to Capital Park shed, Pretoria, for initial test runs over the fearsome gradients of the line to Witbank. Keith Pirt caught up with No. 3450 in August 1983 when the engine was undergoing tests on the Bloemfontein – Kimberley – De Aar lines. Suffice it to say that in general terms, 26 3450 proved itself better in all round performance than any of

the then SAR diesel classes, and most of the electrics too! This is a generalisation of course, but what the tests showed was that with further development, the Class 26 could form the basis of a fleet of steam locomotives unequalled in overall performance and fully justifying their cost, at least in terms of South Africa's situation at the time. But it was not to be and SAR killed off the project, removed many of the "non-standard" improvements – particularly the gas-producer - and basically reduced the engine to a red-painted, somewhat modified Class 25NC. The final insult – in your scribe's opinion anyway – was the change of name to The Red Devil, which appellation the locomotive had gained just about everywhere. Today, (2008) 3450 rests at Dal Josafat, near Cape Town, in a steadily deteriorating condition – a sad end to what could have been a tremendous project.

By May 1984, 26 3450 was based at Kimberley's Beaconsfield shed, being used in the same links as the Class 25NC, on the lines to De Aar and Bloemfontein. Little surprise then, that the loco has a somewhat work-stained condition. *KRP C638*

Ridding itself of any accumulated deposits in the boiler, 26 3450 blows-down, at the towers specifically erected for the purpose, at the exit from De Aar shed. It is August 1983 and the loco is just about to haul another test train. *KRP C627*

Running with the SAR's dynamometer car behind the engine, 26 3450 heads away from Immigrant station in August 1983, with a Kimberley to Bloemfontein freight. That is almost certainly David Wardale himself, leaning out of the cab, trying to ascertain the cause of the uncharacteristic – and unwanted! – smoke emission. *KRP C628*

71

A final look at 26 3450 moving as she was designed to – very swiftly, but very quietly, with little emissions. She hauls the 18-coach De Aar to Kimberley passenger train past the koppie at Behrshoek, August 1983. *KRP 778*